Mathematics for Indian Retail Business

Dr. J. K. Sachdeva
Ph.D., MBA, PGDMM
Director,
NKE Society's
Sri M. Visvesvaraya Institute of
Management Studies and Research (SVIMS)
Wadala (W), Mumbai-400 031.

AND

Abhishek Sachdeva
Manager (Marketing),
Bank of Baroda,
Mumbai.

First Edition: 2011

Himalaya Publishing House

MUMBAI • NEW DELHI • NAGPUR • BENGALURU • HYDERABAD • CHENNAI • PUNE • LUCKNOW • AHMEDABAD • ERNAKULAM • BHUBANESWAR • INDORE • KOLKATA • GUWAHATI

AF633123

© Authors

No part of this publication may be reproduced, stored in a retrieval system, or transmitted in any form or by any means, electronic, mechanical, photocopying, recording and/or otherwise without the prior written permission of the publishers.

First Edition : 2011

Published by : Mrs. Meena Pandey for **Himalaya Publishing House Pvt. Ltd.,**
"Ramdoot", Dr. Bhalerao Marg, Girgaon, **Mumbai - 400 004.**
Phone: 022-23860170/23863863, Fax: 022-23877178
E-mail: himpub@vsnl.com; Website: www.himpub.com

Branch Offices :

New Delhi : "Pooja Apartments", 4-B, Murari Lal Street, Ansari Road, Darya Ganj, New Delhi - 110 002. Phone: 011-23270392, 23278631; Fax: 011-23256286

Nagpur : Kundanlal Chandak Industrial Estate, Ghat Road, Nagpur - 440 018. Phone: 0712-2738731, 3296733; Telefax: 0712-2721215

Bengaluru : No. 16/1 (Old 12/1), 1st Floor, Next to Hotel Highlands, Madhava Nagar, Race Course Road, Bengaluru - 560 001. Phone: 080-32919385; Telefax: 080-22286611

Hyderabad : No. 3-4-184, Lingampally, Besides Raghavendra Swamy Matham, Kachiguda, Hyderabad - 500 027. Phone: 040-27560041, 27550139; Mobile: 09848130433

Chennai : No. 85/50, Bazullah Road, T. Nagar, Chennai - 600 017. Phone: 044-28144004/28144005

Pune : First Floor, "Laksha" Apartment, No. 527, Mehunpura, Shaniwarpeth (Near Prabhat Theatre), Pune - 411 030. Phone: 020-24496323/24496333

Lucknow : Jai Baba Bhavan, Church Road, Near Manas Complex and Dr. Awasthi Clinic, Aliganj, Lucknow - 226 024. Phone: 0522-2339329, 4068914; Mobile: 09305302158, 09415349385, 09389593752

Ahmedabad : 114, "SHAIL", 1st Floor, Opp. Madhu Sudan House, C.G. Road, Navrang Pura, Ahmedabad - 380 009. Phone: 079-26560126; Mobile: 09327324149, 09377088847

Ernakulam : 39/104 A, Lakshmi Apartment, Karikkamuri Cross Rd., Ernakulam, Cochin - 622011, Kerala. Phone: 0484-2378012, 2378016; Mobile: 09344199799

Bhubaneswar : 5 Station Square, Bhubaneswar - 751 001 (Odisha). Phone: 0674-2532129, Mobile: 09861046007

Indore : Kesardeep Avenue Extension, 73, Narayan Bagh, Flat No. 302, IIIrd Floor, Near Humpty Dumpty School, Indore - 452 007 (M.P.). Mobile: 09301386468

Kolkata : 108/4, Beliaghata Main Road, Near ID Hospital, Opp. SBI Bank, Kolkata - 700 010, Phone: 033-32449649, Mobile: 09910440956

Guwahati : House No. 15, Behind Pragjyotish College, Near Sharma Printing Press, P.O. Bharalumukh, Guwahati - 781009, (Assam). Mobile: 09883055590, 09883055536

DTP by : HPH, Editorial Office, Bhandup (Rajani Tambe)

Printed at : **7 Hills Printers**, Hyderabad

PREFACE

A retailer is the final business in a distribution channel. It is interface between customers and the rest of the channel. Thus, retailer is a business that sells products and services to customers for their personal, family or non-business use. Retailing includes all the activities involved in selling goods or services directly to the final consumer for personal or non-business use. Retailing is the sale of goods and services to the ultimate consumer for personal, family household use. Thus, retailing involves more than selling tangible products. It includes every sale of goods and services to the final consumer. Thus purchase of a service such as reservation of railway ticket, consultancy of a physician, maintenance services of a plumber, carpenter, hair-cut etc., dry cleaning, stay at hotel, rental of book, home delivery of goods, consultation by lawyer/doctor are also retail transactions. Consumer is a key issue in the concept of retailing. The person who runs the shop will not be the ultimate or final or 'end of the chain' customers (end user). All retailing do not occur through stores or shops. There are numerous examples of non-store retailing, such of Aquaguard by Eureka Forbes, sale of cosmetics by Avon, catalogue sales by L.L.Bean, etc. Also retailing does not need physical presence of retailer or his representative. For example, automatic vending machines.

Retailing accounts for about 15-20% of the organized workforce in any developed economy. It is the second largest employer in the India after agriculture. There are about 6 million retail establishments in India. Of which, 4.1 million (70%) sell food products and related items. An interesting research in this area has shown that grocery stores (56% of all retail outlets) and general stores (13%) dominate rural India. There are 1.8 million retail outlets in urban India. Of which more than 50% earn between ₹ 7,500 and ₹ 25,000 daily. Approximately 6.6% of urban adults in India are shop owners. There are about 21% outlets in urban area engaged service retailing. Retailing accounts for an impressive part of Gross Domestic Product (GDP).

Cooperative marketing is not new to India. To get the economies of scale, Indian craftsmen and traders made shrenies or groups of similar products and trade during 6th and 7th centuries. This was the basis of caste system. The villages during medieval and British period grew with cooperative trade. Cooperative marketing is just an extension and application of the philosophy of cooperation in the area of agricultural marketing. It is a process of marketing through a cooperative society, formed for the producers, by the producers. It seeks to eliminate the middlemen between the producer and the consumer, thus getting the maximum price for their produce. Kirana shops are traditional retail outlets in India. However with the advent of new cooperative marketing with modern all facility malls, there is general perception that retails consumers are getting skewed towards malls and consequently Kirana stores are experiencing tough competition to retain their customers.

India is witnessing a change in the age and income profiles of its over 1 billion population, which is likely to fuel accelerated consumption in the years to come.

The country is believed to have an average age of 24 years for its population as against 36 years for the USA and 30 years for China. A younger population tends to have higher aspirations and spends more as it enters the earning phase. Besides, the gradual disintegration of the traditional Indian joint family system has led to nuclearisation of families, which in turn has led to enhanced demand. Add to this an increasing population of working women and new job opportunities in emerging service sectors such as IT-enabled services, retail, food services, entertainment and financial services.

Retailer is a marketer who decides about products to be sold, price the consumer may demand and work on sales promotion techniques. While deciding prices, he should know the basic techniques of calculating the mark ups/down, discounts, profits etc.

Retail mathematics is not a new branch of learning and I am not the first person to write on the subject. Theoretical examples are based on the broad range of writings on the subject. Some of the examples will not be novel, as they have been dealt with elsewhere by many authors. However, my point is to put the things in a simple way so that students may understand in easy way. Though a unique way has been adopted while presenting the topics, I shall not deny that authors, whom I have referred, have already contributed a lot to the subject. I am humbly presenting the subject.

Major techniques used in retail have been discussed in the chapters like merchandising for profits, structuring price lines, inventory planning and control, invoicing etc. Students of retail management have been encouraged to calculate by heart. A chapter on regression for small business is an add on.

Abhishek Sachdeva has contributed a lot in designing the chapter plan and adding contents in each chapter which a retail manager should know.

Nothing is perfect in this world and there are always chances to improve. Suggestions are sought from students and teachers. I shall always remain obliged for any improvement suggestions.

J. K. Sachdeva

9892728281

sachdevajk@hotmail.com

DETAILED CONTENTS

CHAPTER 1

Merchandising for Profit

1.1 LEARNING OBJECTIVES

After reading this chapter you will be able to know:

1. Meaning of profit, profit factor and Profit and Loss statement
2. Concept of fixed costs, variable cost and break-even point
3. Concepts of Gross sales, cost of goods sold, profit margin and customer' returns and allowances
4. How to increase profits?

1.2 PROFIT FACTORS

Introduction - The Meaning of Profit

The starting point in understanding the profit and loss account is to be clear about the meaning of "**profit**".

Profit is the **incentive** for business; without profit people do not work. Profit is the reward for taking risk; generally speaking high risk = high reward (or loss if it goes wrong) and low risk = low reward. People won't take risks without reward. All business is risky (some more than others) so no reward means no business. No business means no jobs, no salaries and no goods and services.

Profit also has an important role in **allocating resources** (land, labour, capital and enterprise). Put simply, falling profits signal that resources should be taken out of that business and put into another one; rising profits signal that resources should be moved into this business. Without these signals we are left to guess as to what is the best use of society's scarce resources.

1.3 PROFIT AND LOSS STATEMENTS

The main task of accounts is to monitor and measure profits.

Profit = Revenue less Costs

So monitoring profit also means monitoring and measuring revenue and costs. There are two parts to this:

(1) **Recording financial data**. This is the 'book-keeping' part of accounting.

(2) **Measuring the result.** This is the 'financial' part of accounting. If we say 'profits are high' this begs the question 'high compared to what?' This is what we read during Ratio Analysis.

Profits are 'spent' in three ways.

(1) **Retained** for future investment and growth.

(2) **Returned** to owners in the form of 'dividend' or profit share.

(3) **Paid** as tax.

1.3.1 Parts of the Profit and Loss Account

The Profit & Loss Account aims to monitor profit. It has three parts.

(1) The Trading Account: This records the money in (revenue) and out (costs) of the business as a result of the business' 'trading' ie buying and selling. This might be buying raw materials and selling finished goods; it might be buying goods wholesale and selling them retail. The figure at the end of this section is the **Gross Profit**.

(2) The Profit and Loss Account proper: This starts with the Gross Profit and adds to it any further costs and revenues, including overheads. These further costs and revenues are from any other activities not directly related to trading. An example is income received from investments.

(3) The Appropriation Account: This shows how the profit is 'appropriated' or divided between the three uses mentioned above.

1.3.2 Uses of the Profit and Loss Account

(1) The main use is to monitor and measure profit, as discussed above. This assumes that the information recording is accurate. Significant problems can arise if the information is inaccurate, either through incompetence or deliberate fraud.

(2) Once the profit (loss) has been accurately calculated, this can then be used for comparison i.e., judging how well the business is doing compared to itself in the past, compared to the managers' plans and compared to other businesses.

(3) There are ways to 'fix' accounts. Internal accounts are rarely 'fixed', because there is little point in the managers fooling themselves (unless fraud is going on) but public accounts are routinely 'fixed' to create a good impression out to the outside world. If you understand accounts, you can usually (not always) spot these 'fixes' and take them out to get a true picture.

Example Profit and Loss Account

An example profit and loss account is provided below:

	₹'000	₹'000
Revenue	12,500	10,000
Cost of Sales	7,500	6,000
Gross Profit	**5,000**	**4,000**
Gross Profit Margin *(gross profit/revenue)*	40%	40%
Operating Costs		
Sales and Distribution	1,260	1,010
Finance and Administration	570	555
Other Overheads	970	895
Depreciation	235	210
Total Operating Costs	3,035	2,670
Operating Profit *(gross profit less operating costs)*	1,965	1,330
Operating Profit Margin *(operating profit/revenue)*	15.7%	13.3%
Interest	(450)	(475)
Profit before Tax	1,515	855
Taxation	(455)	(255)
Profit after Tax	1,060	600
Dividends	650	400
Retained Profits	410	200

The contents analysis of the profit and loss account covers several aspects: horizontal analysis, vertical analysis, calculation of economic and financial indicators.

1.3.3 The Horizontal Analysis of the Profit and Loss Account

The horizontal analysis of the profit and loss account has as finality the calculation of variation in time of the components that have influenced the evolution of the financial results, which is the company's revenues and expenditures in total, but also the three types of activities:

operating, financial and extraordinary. The research involves systematization, and the determination of the index variation. The research of the above elements gives the opportunity to characterize the evolution of the results' definitive elements. Calculations show if the revenues dynamics exceeds the expenditures one, which is the dynamic results for the three types of activities that they generate.

1.3.4 The Vertical Analysis of the Profit and Loss Account

The vertical analysis is useful because it helps calculating the intermediary sold of administration and the provisional estimation of the operating outcome. Analysis of the company's results based on grouping revenues and expenditures by their nature offers the ability to calculate the intermediate balance administration, which, to some extent, is a variant of the profit and loss account. By reporting each category of expenditure in the turnover (raw materials, materials, labor personnel expenditures and amortization), it is obtained their ratio in the turnover. When there are no major changes in the company's activity, the above calculations represent a relatively easy way to predict the elements of profit and loss account by applying the ratio of the above elements on the estimated turnover.

1.4 CONCEPT OF BREAK-EVEN POINT

First we shall have to understand the concept of Break-Even Analysis

Break-even analysis is a technique widely used by production management and management accountants. However, it is widely used by retailers also. It is based on categorising procurement costs between those which are "variable" (costs that change when the quantity of sales changes) and those that are "fixed" (costs not directly related to the volume of sale).

Total variable and fixed costs are compared with sales revenue in order to determine the **level of sales volume, sales value or production at which the business makes neither a profit nor a loss (the "break-even point").**

1.4.1 The Break-Even Chart

In its simplest form, the break-even chart is a graphical representation of costs at various levels of activity shown on the same chart as the variation of income (or sales, revenue) with the same variation in activity. The point at which neither profit nor loss is made is known as the "break-even point" and is represented on the chart below by the intersection of the two lines:

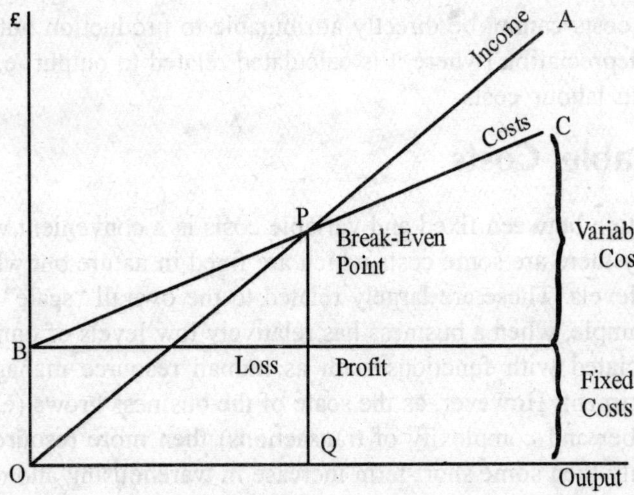

In the diagram above, the line OA represents the variation of income at varying levels of production activity ("output"). OB represents the total fixed costs in the business. As output increases, variable costs are incurred, meaning that total costs (fixed + variable) also increase. At low levels of output, Costs are greater than Income. At the point of intersection, P, costs are exactly equal to income, and hence neither profit nor loss is made.

1.4.2 Fixed Costs

Fixed costs are those business costs that are not directly related to the level of production or output. In other words, even if the business has a zero output or high output, the level of fixed costs will remain broadly the same. In the long term fixed costs can alter – perhaps as a result of investment in production capacity (e.g., adding a new factory unit) or through the growth in overheads required to support a larger, more complex business.

Examples of fixed costs:

- Rent and rates
- Depreciation
- Telephone fixed bills
- Marketing costs (non-revenue related)
- Administration costs

1.4.3 Variable Costs

Variable costs are those costs which vary directly with the level of sales. A distinction is often made between **"Direct"** variable costs and **"Indirect"** variable costs.

Direct variable costs are those which can be directly attributable to the production of a particular product or service and allocated to a particular cost centre. Raw materials and the wages those working on the production line are good examples.

Indirect variable costs cannot be directly attributable to production but they do vary with output. These include depreciation (where it is calculated related to output e.g. machine hours), maintenance and certain labour costs.

1.4.4 Semi-Variable Costs

Whilst the distinction between fixed and variable costs is a convenient way of categorising business costs, in reality there are some costs which are fixed in nature but which increase when output reaches certain levels. These are largely related to the overall "scale" and/or complexity of the business. For example, when a business has relatively low levels of output or sales, it may not require costs associated with functions such as human resource management or a fully-resourced finance department. However, as the scale of the business grows (e.g., output, number people employed, number and complexity of transactions) then more resources are required. If production rises suddenly then some short-term increase in warehousing and/or transport may be required. In these circumstances, we say that part of the cost is variable and part fixed.

The **break-even point** for a product is the point where total revenue received equals the total costs associated with the sale of the product

TR = TC

A break-even point is typically calculated in order for businesses to determine if it would be profitable to sell a proposed product, as opposed to attempting to modify an existing product instead so it can be made lucrative. Break-even analysis can also be used to analyse the potential profitability of an expenditure in a sales-based business.

break even point = fixed cost/contribution per unit

contribution (p.u) = selling price (p.u) – variable cost (p.u)

break even point (for sales) = fixed cost/contribution (pu) * sp (pu)

Here we can say contribution is retailer's margin.

For instance, a retailer gets a product from the distributor or wholesale price at a price of ₹ 80 and the sale price is ₹ 100. So the product contribution is ₹ 20. The shopkeeper spends ₹ 10,000 as fixed costs in month. It means shopkeeper will have to sell (10,000/20) = 500 units to break-even. His profit can start if he sells 501 units or more. Now a shopkeeper usually sell many more products in shop, he can allocate the share of Fixed Costs to each product.

1.4.5 Margin of Safety

Margin of safety represents the strength of the business. It enables a business man to know that what is the exact amount he/she has gained or loss over or below break even point).

Margin of safety = ((sales – break-even sales)/sales) × 100% If P/V ratio is given then sales/pv ratio

1.4.6 Limitations

- Break-even analysis is only a supply side (i.e., costs only) analysis, as it tells you nothing about what sales are actually likely to be for the product at these various prices.
- It assumes that fixed costs (FC) are constant
- It assumes average variable costs are constant per unit of output, at least in the range of likely quantities of sales. (i.e., linearity)
- It assumes that the quantity of goods produced is equal to the quantity of goods sold (i.e., there is no change in the quantity of goods held in inventory at the beginning of the period and the quantity of goods held in inventory at the end of the period).
- In multi-product companies, it assumes that the relative proportions of each product sold and produced are constant (i.e., the sales mix is constant).

1.5 ACTIVITY BASED PRICING

Activity based pricing (ABP) is a pricing method that uses knowledge about customer demand and knowledge about the costs of a specific selling situation to establish a price that will result in a specific planned profit. Market research can estimate the amount of product that will be sold at various prices. Activity based costing allows the company to project costs corresponding to various sales volumes. When this information is combined, the company can project total revenue, expenses, and profit at any point on the customer demand curve. This process is called ABP. Activity based pricing is important because it marries volume sensitive marketing data with volume sensitive cost accounting to provide definitive answers about pricing. Market research data, when used alone, can project the price at which revenue is maximized, but not the price at which profit is maximized. Cost accounting data, when viewed without marketing data, tell how many units the company would have to sell at various prices to earn a profit, but provides no insight into how many units customers will buy. When both customer demand and cost are analyzed together, ABP can provide definitive answers about price. When activity based costing data and customer demand data for many customers are combined, an analysis shows that in real world situations profit is maximized at a price that is always higher than the price that maximizes revenues.

Activity based pricing provides a competitive advantage to companies that use it. This technique does not promise that a company using ABP will have big increases in sales. Many companies could quickly achieve large sales increases by simply lowering price. However, major price reductions are usually a formula for disastrous financial performance. ABP is a strategy for superior financial performance through superior financial knowledge. A company that uses ABP will often be able to win competitively bid contracts for desirable high volume work when competing against companies using more traditional pricing methods.

There are four commandments of ABP. They relate to required knowledge about both revenue and expenses. These commandments are:

1. Know thy product.
2. Know thy processes.
3. Know thy customers.
4. Know thy competitors.

Marketing people have long known how to estimate how many units of a product would be sold at various price points. Unfortunately, for a long time marketing's ability to accurately describe the behaviour of the revenue side of the profit equation surpassed the ability of cost accounting to model the behaviour of costs. Despite these shortcomings, cost accounting personnel still usually gave management a single number that represented cost and was able to convince everyone they knew what they were doing.

In order to perform ABP (Activity based process), a company must be able to take the activity costs that have been derived through its activity-based costing efforts and recombine them based on the resources that a new product is expected to consume.

Many businesses give discounts to their customers based on the volume of product that they purchase. Some companies define their discount based on the number of units of a particular product that are purchased, others provide a discount based on the value of all items purchased in one order, while still others consider the total amount of purchases that the customer buys for the whole year. A customer's buying pattern affects the cost to serve that customer. The way that a discount schedule is structured also may affect the manner in which a customer makes its purchases.

Price influences the volume of product that will be sold. In general, as price increases, sales volume decreases. Sales volume affects product costs; therefore, costs can only be stated accurately for a specific number of units. ABP seeks to identify the appropriate price to charge for a product based on a specific situation.

Costs are often categorized as fixed, variable, and step-variable. Most products have costs that fall into all three categories. Because of fixed costs and step variable costs, unit costs decrease as sales volume increases. Costs may be customer related as well as product related. Accordingly, different prices may be appropriate for different customers or categories of cus-tomers.. In the real world, when selling a product that will be purchased by many customers, the price that maximizes profit is higher than the price that maximizes.

1.6 BASIC ELEMENTS OF PROFIT IN RETAIL

The function of the retail store is to sell merchandise to consumers at a profit. These sales are the store's source of operating income. Before merchandise can be sold, however, it must be bought. Even in a computerized organization in which financial personnel may preset programs and spreadsheets, the buyer is ultimately responsible for creating a merchandise assortment. This selection occurs after planning and predicting what, when, where, and how much to buy and what to pay for these purchases. Cost is the amount the retailer pays for these purchases. Retail is the price at which stores offer merchandise for sale to the consumer.

Profit and Loss statement is used to measure profitability as it evaluates the results of current performance and allows for comparison of present and possible future trends. Because the buyer buys and prices the merchandise offered for sale in a retail store, the buyer must have the ability to know, manipulate, and understand the interaction among the three basic profit factors, which are: the operating income, also known as sales or sales volume, which indicates in rupee s how much merchandise has been sold; the cost of goods sold, which shows the amount paid for the goods sold; and the operating expenses, which refers to those expenses, other than the cost of the goods, incurred in the buying/selling process.

Gross sales are the entire amount received for goods sold during a given period. This total sales figure is calculated by multiplying the retail price of the individual items of merchandise by the number of pieces actually sold to consumers. The accurate calculation of gross sales, however, must also take into account adjustments because of returns and price reductions. Stores typically give customers the privilege of returning merchandise. When merchandise is returned to stock and the customer receives a cash refund or a charge credit, these returns of sales are called customer returns. In addition, if a customer receives a price reduction after the sale is completed, it is known as a customer allowance. These two adjustments are referred to collectively as customer returns and allowances. When a customer return or allowance takes place, the previously recorded sale must be cancelled and subtracted from the gross sales amount. When customer returns and allowances are subtracted from gross sales, the resulting total is the net sales figure. Thus, net sales is the sales total after customer returns and allowances have been deducted from gross sales. Net sales represent the amount of goods that actually stay sold. When retailers calculate profit, the net sales figure is the more significant because a firm can only realize a profit on goods that remain sold at the retail price. For this reason, the term sales volume is always a net sales figure.

Merchandisers must determine and balance the retail price for the items they purchase for sale to customers with, among other factors, how much they can afford to pay a vendor for merchandise. Cost of goods sold is simply the cost of the merchandise that has been sold during a given time period. This concept is simple, but the actual calculation is complex because other necessary adjustments must be made to the cost or purchase price that appears on the bill or invoice (vendor's bill). These adjustments are transportation costs, known as inward freight, which is the amount a vendor may charge for transporting merchandise to the designated premises of the retailer; alteration and workroom costs, which is a chaise to a selling department when it is necessary to treat merchandise so that it will be in condition for sale (i.e., assembling, polish-ing, making cuffs, etc.); and cash discounts, which vendors may grant for payment of an invoice within a specified period of time.

In addition, the retailer must maintain a place of business from which die goods are sold, and to maintain this place, it must incur operating expense. Operating expenses usually fall into two major categories and are charged to a merchandise department to determine the net profit for that department. Expenses that are specific to a given department and that would cease if that department were discontinued are called direct expenses. These include salaries of the buyer, assistant buyer, and salespeople; departmental advertising; selling supplies; and customer delivery expenses. Store expenses that exist whether a department is added to or discontinued are indirect expenses. These include store expenses that are prorated to all selling departments on the basis of their sales volume, such as store maintenance, insurance, and salaries of top management.

1.7 ELEMENTS OF EACH BASIC PROFIT FACTOR

Each of the basic profit factors needs to be dissected because each consists of elements that contribute to profit. The calculations involved highlight the meaning and importance of each element.

1.7.1 Operating Income (Sales)

Gross Sales

Gross sales are the total initial rupees received for merchandise sold during a given period.

CONCEPT:

Gross sales = Total of all the prices charged to consumers on individual items × Number of units actually sold.

Solved Example

On Monday, an accessories department sold 30 dolls priced at ₹ 15 each, 25 dolls priced at ₹ 25 each, and 5 dolls priced at ₹ 30 each. What were the gross sales for that day?

Solution:

30 dolls @ ₹ 15 each = ₹ 450

5 dolls @ ₹ 30 each = 150

25 dolls @ ₹ 25 each = 625

Gross sales = ₹ 1,225

1.7.2 Customer Returns and Allowances

Customer returns and allowances are profit factors because the customer receives either a complete refund of the purchase price or a partial rebate. Thus, the retailer must make a corresponding deduction from the gross sales figure because these transactions result in some cancellation of sales. This rupee figure is usually expressed as a percentage of gross sales.

Customer returns and allowances = Total of all refunds or credits to the customer on individual items of merchandise × Number of units actually returned.

1.7.2.1 Solved Example

On Saturday, the junior petite department refunded ₹ 98 for one velour jacket, ₹ 75 each for two wool skirts, and ₹ 55 each for two velvet tops. Other returns for the week amounted to ₹ 400, and the weekly total of allowances given was ₹ 57. What was the rupee amount of customer returns and allowances?

Solution:

Valour Jacket = ₹ 98

Wool skirts = ₹ 150

Velvet Tops = ₹ 110

Customer Returns for Saturday = 358

Total weekly returns = ₹ 400

Total weekly allowance = ₹ 57

Customer returns and allowance for week = ₹ 815

Customer returns and allowance percentage = The sum of customer returns and allowances expressed as a percentage of gross sales.

Customer returns and allowances % = Customer returns and allowances/Gross sales

1.7.2.2 Solved Example

Last week, the junior petite sportswear department had gross sales of ₹ 20,375. Customer returns and allowances for the week totalled ₹ 815. What was the combined percentage of allowances and merchandise returns for the week?

Solution:

Customer returns and allowances % = 815/20,375

Customer returns and allowances % = 4%

Conversely, customer returns and allowances can be computed when the gross sales and customer returns and allowances percentage are known.

Customer returns and allowances = Gross sales × Customer returns and allowances percentage.

1.7.2.3 Solved Example

Last week, the junior petite sportswear department reported gross sales of ₹ 20,375, with customer returns and allowances of 4%. What was the rupee amount of customer returns and allowances?

Solution:

Rupee customer returns and allowances = ₹ 20,375 gross sales × 4% customer returns and allowances

Rupee customer returns and allowances = ₹ 815

1.7.3 Net Sales

Net sales are the sales total for a given period after customer returns and allowances have been deducted from gross sales.

Net sales = Gross sales – Customer returns and allowances.

1.7.3.1 Solved Example

A housewares department sold ₹ 65,000 worth of merchandise. Customer returns were ₹ 6,500. What were the net sales of this department?

Solution:

Gross sales = Net sales – Customer returns and allowances

= ₹ 65,000 – 6,500 = ₹ 58,500

In retailing, the operating income is known as net sales. The net sales figure, also called sales volume, is used to designate the size of a particular store or a merchandise department. Retailers use net sales to measure a department's performance or productivity. It is common practice to calculate the percentage of sales that an individual department has contributed to the store's net sales. This type of analysis allows a retailer to compare a particular department of one store with other departments or stores within the company, as well as to compare this selected department's sales with industry figures.

The individual department's net sales are expressed as a percentage of the store's total net sales.

Department's net sales % of total store sales = Department's net sales/Store's total net rupee sales

1.7.3.2 Solved Example

The costume jewellery department had net sales of ₹ 9,00,000. For the same period, total store sales were ₹ 4,50,00,000. What is the costume jewellery department's net sales percentage of the total store's net sales?

Solution:

Department's net sales = ₹ 9,00,000

Total store net sales = ₹ 4,50,00,000

Department's net sales % of total store sales = 2%

Because net sales are determined by the adjustment of customer returns and allowances to gross sales, it is also possible through this relationship to calculate, when desired, a gross sales amount—provided an amount of the net sales and the percentage of customer returns and allowances are known.

Gross sales = Net sales/100% (Gross sales) – Customer returns and allowances%

1.7.3.3 Solved Example

The net sales of a Department were ₹ 4,60,000. The customer returns and allowances were 8%. What were the gross sales of the department?

Solution:

4,60,000/(100 – 8) = ₹ 5,00,000

1.7.4 Cost of Merchandise Sold

The control of the cost of goods sold is crucial to profitability. The buyer, who decides what merchandise to buy, also makes decisions regarding the cost, transportation, and credit terms as they relate to these purchases. In actual practice, to determine the accurate cost of goods sold, there must be a complete calculation to represent the total cost of goods purchased, which begins with an invoice or billed cost to which the following factors are adjusted:

Billed cost is the purchase price that appears on the invoice (i.e., vendor's bill)

PLUS

Inward freight or transportation costs.

This is the amount that a vendor may charge for delivery of merchandise. Inward freight plus billed cost is called the billed delivered cost.

PLUS

Alteration and workroom costs.

It is accepted practice to treat this figure as an additional cost because it applies only to merchandise that has been sold and not to all purchases.

MINUS

Cash discounts.

These are discounts that vendors may grant for payment of an invoice within a specified time. For example, a vendor may offer a 2% cash discount (deducted from the billed cost) if payment is made within a designated time period. The discounts are offered in the form of a percentage and are deducted from only the billed cost, but the rupee discount earned is used in the calculation of the total cost of sales. For example, a 2% cash discount given on a billed cost of ₹ 1,000 translates into a ₹ 20 deduction:

₹ 1,000 billed cost × 2% cash discount

cash discount = ₹ 20

Concept

Total cost of merchandise = Billed cost + Inward transportation charges – Workroom costs – Cash discount.

1.7.4.1 Solved Example

An activewear department, for a six-month period, had billed costs of merchandise amounting to ₹ 80,000; transportation charges of ₹ 2,000; earned cash discounts of 7 1/2%, and workroom costs of ₹ 500. Calculate the total cost of merchandise.

Solution:

Billed costs	+ ₹ 80,000
Inward freight	+ ₹ 2,000
Billed delivered cost	₹ 82,000
+ Workroom costs	+ ₹ 500
Gross merchandise costs	₹ 82,500
– Cash discount \	
(7 1/2% × ₹ 80,000)	– 6,000
Total cost of merchandise	₹ 76,500

1.7.5 Operating Expenses

Because the expenses of operating a business determine whether or not a net profit is achieved, the control and management of operating expenses are of major concern. For the purpose of analysis, the expenses incurred by the retailer (e.g., maintenance of store space, salaries, etc.) are classified to measure the performance of the designated function or activity. There are various approaches to classifying these items and, although there are many different kinds of expenses, each can be easily identified as just that. However, there is a variation in the format used to record them. Traditionally, operating expenses fall into two major categories and are charged to a merchandise department to determine its net profit. These major categories are direct and indirect expenses.

1.7.6 Direct Expenses

Direct expenses exist only within a given department and cease if that department is discontinued. These might include salespeople's and buyers' salaries, buyers' travelling expenses, advertising, selling supplies, delivery to customers, and selling space. For the purpose of expense analysis in retailing, the amount of floor space occupied that generates a given department's sales volume is allotted by the square foot and is charged directly to that department even though there is no cash outlay. Each expense and/or the total direct expenses are expressed as a percentage of net sales. For example, if the net sales of a department are ₹ 1,00,000 and ₹ 3,500 is spent on advertising, the percentage of advertising expenses would be ₹ 3,500 ÷ ₹ 100,000, or 3.5%.

1.7.7 Indirect Expenses

Indirect expenses are store expenses that will continue to exist even if the particular department is discontinued. These might include store maintenance, insurance, security, depreciation of equipment, and salaries of senior executives. Many indirect expenses are distributed among individual departments on the basis of its sales volume (e.g., if a department contributes 1.5% to the store's total sales, the indirect expenses charged to this department are 1.5%).

Operating expenses = Direct expenses + Indirect expenses

1.7.7.1 Solved Example

A children's department has net sales of ₹ 3,00,000, and indirect expenses are 10% of net sales. Direct expenses are:

- Selling salaries = ₹ 24,000
- Advertising expenses = 6,000
- Buying salaries = 12,000
- Other direct expenses = 18,000

Find the total operating expenses of the department in rupees and as a percentage.

Solution:

Indirect expenses (10% × ₹ 3,00,000) = ₹ 30,000 Direct expenses:

Selling salaries = 24,000

Advertising = 6,000

Buying salaries = 12,000

Other = 18,000

Total operating expenses = ₹ 90,000

Operating expense %

90,000/3,00,000*100 = 30%

1.7.8 Controllable and Non-controllable Expenses

There are additional expenses that further complicate expense assignments. Many, but not all, direct expenses are controllable expenses. For example, the rent for branch store Y is directly related to this store, but is not under the control of the present store manager because this expense was previously negotiated. Utilities are another example of a direct expense to a store, but an indirect expense to a particular department. The rates are not controllable, but the utilization is.

Because retailers do not always agree on the handling of expenses, some firms use the contribution technique to evaluate the performance of a buyer or store manager. Contribution, also known as controllable margin, includes those expenses that are direct, controllable, or a combination of direct and controllable (e.g., selling salaries).

Contribution is the amount the department contributes to indirect expenses and profit as shown below

		Rupees	%age	
Net Sales		₹ 5,00,000	100.0%	
(minus) Cost of Merch. Sold		–2,66,000	–53.2%	
		₹ 2,34,000	46.8%	
(minus) Direct Expenses				
Payroll	₹ 73,000			
Advertising	13,000			
Supplies	7,000			
Travel	5,000			
Other	12,000			
		–1,10,000	–22.0%	₹ 1,10,000
				₹ 5,00,000
Contribution		1,24,000	24.8%	₹ 1,24,000
				₹ 5,00,000
(minus) Indirect Expenses		1,06,500	21.3%	₹ 1,06,500
				₹ 5,00,000
Operating Profit		₹ 17,500	3.5%	

1.8 THE RELATIONSHIPS AMONG THE BASIC PROFIT FACTORS

The following examples show the relationships among the **three fundamental factors** on which the amount of profit depends. For comparison, these factors are expressed in percentages as well as in amount. The net sales figure is the basis for determining profit computation, and so is considered 100%. The other factors involved are shown and stated as a percentage of net sales.

Example:

Net sales (operating income) say ₹ 10,000 (100%)

Cost of Merchandise sold say ₹ 5,500 (55%)

Operating expenses. say ₹ 4,300 (43%)

Profit ₹ 200 (2%)

From the break-even analysis, we can say that there are only three ways to increase profit:

- Increase your sales volumes.
- Increase your sales prices.
- Reduce your costs.

Use 7ps techniques to increase sales volume and sales price. Negotiate with manufacturers, wholesalers and distributors for better retail margins.

The factors that govern profits are variable and net profits do not represent any fixed sum. As a frame of reference, Following table lists various types of retail stores and their profit performances. These results illustrate that the amount of profit generated can be different depending on the type of organization and is rarely, if ever, constant. For each store type, the actual figures will change annually, but the information required for analysis will remain constant.

After reviewing a profit and loss statement, however, to determine how each of these factors affects profit, certain measures can be taken to improve profits. However, because these three factors (that is, sales, cost of goods sold, and operating expenses) are always interrelated, the adjustments made must keep all three factors balanced in relationship to one another. Fundamentally, profits can be improved through the following three approaches:

1. Increase sales with only a proportionate increase in the cost of the merchandise and little or no increase in expenses.
2. Decrease the cost of merchandise sold without a decrease in sales (e.g., sell a larger proportion of higher markup merchandise or decrease the net cost of goods sold by lowering shipping charges and/or obtaining greater cash discounts).
3. Reduce expenses.

Profit Performance by Store Type

Store Type	Profits			Profits to Sales	
Last Year	This Year	% Change	Last Year	This Year	
Department stores	₹ 14,70,655	₹ 15,80,722	+ 7.5	3.3%	3.5%
Mass merchandisers	18,96,700	20,33,300	+ 7.1	2.8	2.8
Specialty stores	5,55,579	5,68,774	+ 2.4	4.4	5.0
Discount stores	3,35,336	4,32,774	+ 29.1	3.4	3.3
Off-price stores	24,143	32,073	+ 32.9	5.4	5.2
Miscellaneous	4,78,326	4,61,537	− 3.5	2.3	2.6
Total	₹ 47,62,739	₹ 51,09,000	+ 7.3	3.0%	3.2%

1.9.1 Solved Example

The following example shows the application and effect of each approach. For the accounting period under consideration, a merchant estimated sales at ₹ 1,00,000, merchandise purchases at ₹ 70,000, and total operating expenses at ₹ 25,000. If the merchant wants to increase the previous 5% net profit, which approach should he take?

Actual Estimated Performance

Sales – Cost of goods sold	= ₹ 1,00,000 – 70,000
Gross margin	= 30,000 = 30%
– Operating expenses	– 25,000 = 25%
Net profit	= ₹ 5,000 = 5%

Method 1:

Increase sales with only a proportionate increase in cost of goods sold and little or no increase in expenses.

Let sales be increased by 10% = 1,10,000

Cost of goods sold 70% = 77,000

Operating Expenses = 25,000

(Increased net profit) = 1,10,000 – 77,000 – 25,000 = 8,000 = 8% (increased by 3%)

Method 2:

Decrease the cost of goods sold without decreasing sales, which is equivalent to a larger gross margin.

Let sales be = 1,00,000

Cost of goods sold 69.5% = 69,500

Operating Expenses = 25,000 Gross margin = 30,500 – Operating expenses – 25,000

Net profit

= ₹ 5,500 = 5.5% (Increased net profit)

Method 3:

Reduce expenses

Decrease the cost of goods sold without decreasing sales, which is equivalent to a larger gross margin.

Let sales be = 1,00,000

Cost of goods sold 70% = 70,000

Operating Expenses = 24,000

Net profit = Gross margin = 30,000 – Operating expenses – 24,000 = ₹ 6,000

6% (Increased net profit by 1%)

1.10 PROBLEMS FOR PRACTICE

1. Customer returns and allowances for department came to ₹ 4,500. Gross sales in the department were ₹ 90,000. What percentage of merchandise sold was returned?
2. The gross sales for store B were ₹ 8,76,500. The customer returns and allowances were 10%.

   (a) What was the rupee amount of returns and allowances?

   (b) What were net sales?
3. The net sales of department X were ₹ 46,780. The customer returns were ₹ 2,342. What were gross sales?
4. For this year, department store G's sales volume was ₹ 55,00,00,000. The junior dress department had net sales of ₹ 82,50,000, and the misses dress department had net sales of ₹ 2,47,50,000. What were the net sales percentages of each department to the total store?
5. Branch store H had total sales of ₹ 3,00,00,000. The hosiery departments sales were 1.9% of store H's total sales. The handbag department's sales were 2.1% of the total branch sales. What were the rupee net sales for each department?
6. Discussion Problem: Explain why a merchant should be alarmed if customer returns are excessive. How does a merchant determine what is an excessive percentage of returns? What can be done by the department itself to correct a problem rate of returns?
7. A gift shop has workroom costs of ₹ 575. The billed cost of merchandise sold amounted to ₹ 59,000, with cash discounts earned of ₹ 1,180, and freight charges of ₹ 650. Find the total cost of the merchandise.

8. A specialty dress shop made purchases amounting to ₹ 3,700 at cost, with 8% cash discounts earned, workroom costs of ₹ 100, and no transportation charges. Determine the total cost of the merchandise.

9. A sporting goods buyer placed the following order:
   - 18 nylon backpacks costing ₹ 22 each
   - 12 two-person tents costing ₹ 54 each
   - 6 camp stoves costing ₹ 55 each.

Shipping costs, paid by the store, were ₹ 60 and a cash discount of 1% was taken. Find:

(a) Billed cost on the total order.

(b) Total delivered cost of the merchandise.

10. Note the following figures:

Net profit 2.5%

Gross margin ₹ 7,000

Operating expenses 6,600

(a) The cost of goods in rupees.

(b) The percentage of operating expenses.

11. The net profit in an appliance of department for the Spring/Summer period was ₹ 20,000, which represented 2% of net sales. Operating expenses totalled ₹ 4,80,000. Find:

(a) The rupee amount of gross margin.

(b) The net sales figure.

12. The linen department had net sales of ₹ 80,000. There was a 2% loss, and the gross margin was 46%. Determine the operating expenses of the department and express the result in rupees and as a percentage.

13. During the year, a stationery store achieved the following results:

Sales	₹ 5,85,000
Purchases, at cost	5,48,000
Transportation charges	5,000
Inventories at cost:	
Beginning of year	5,55,000
End of year	5,00,000

Determine the gross cost of merchandise sold.

14. Find the net profit or loss as a percentage and the gross margin as a amount:

Gross sales	₹ 2,00,000
Customer returns and allowances	15,000
Opening inventory, at cost	38,000
Billed cost of goods	99,000
Inward transportation	5,000
Cash discount	6,000
Closing inventory, at cost	36,000
Payroll	48,000
Occupancy	28,000
Wrapping and packing	1,200
Utilities	2,000
Delivery	2,800

15. Construct a profit and loss statement using the following departmental figures and show the amounts for net sales, total cost of goods sold, gross margin, expenses, and profit:

Gross sales	₹ 82,000
Customer returns and allowances	4,000
Inward freight	2,000
Workroom costs	1,000
Opening inventory, at cost	17,000
Closing inventory, at cost	14,000
Purchases, at cost	36,000
Cash discounts	8%
Advertising	5,000
Rent	12,000
Salaries	17,000
Miscellaneous expenses	2,500

16. Construct a final profit and loss statement from the figures listed below and calculate the major factors as percentages and rupee amounts.

Opening inventory	₹ 74,200
Gross sales	2,48,000
Advertising	15,000
Misc. expenses	18,000
Purchases, at cost	1,20,000
Closing inventory	78,000
Customer returns	25,800
Salaries	26,000
Transportation charges	8,000
Rent	39,000
Cash discounts	3%

17. The following figures are for your department:

Net sales	₹ 4,90,000
Billed cost of goods	2,65,000
Freight charges	11,160
Rent	56,640
Salaries	1,11,600
Miscellaneous expenses	25,260
Cash discounts	37,000
Insurance	27,800
Advertising	16,740
Opening inventory (cost)	1,17,000
Closing inventory (cost)	1,20,000

(a) Calculate the total cost of goods sold.

(b) Determine the operating expenses in rupees.

(c) Determine the profit or loss in rupee s and as a percentage.

18. If profit is ₹ 8,000 and profit percentage is 4%, what is the net sales figure?

19. If expenses are ₹ 85,340 and gross margin is ₹ 90,960, express operating profit or loss in rupees.

20. Find the net profit or loss in rupees and as a percentage if:

Opening inventory (cost)	₹ 70,000
Operating expenses	1,80,000
Closing inventory	72,000
Net sales	4,00,000
Inward freight	5,000
Purchases, at cost	2,10,000

21. Gross sales are ₹ 25,619; customer returns and allowances are ₹ 2,791.32; purchases at billed cost are ₹ 12,585; inward freight is ₹ 932.45; and cash discounts earned average 2%. What is the gross margin in rupees?

22. If a department experiences a loss of 3% during a six-month period and its gross margin is 43%, what must its expense percentage be?

23. Gross margin in the shoe department was ₹ 1,85,000. Operating expenses were ₹ 1,78,000, and the net profit was 2% of net sales. What were the net sales?

23. Express the gross margin as a percentage if:

Gross sales	₹ 2,83,000
Customer returns	7,000
Billed cost of goods	1,37,000
Inward freight	5,000
Workroom charges	3,000
Cash discounts	6%

24. Find the gross margin percentage when:

Gross sales	₹ 5,66,000
Customer returns	10%
Billed cost of goods	2,58,000
Inward freight	9,000
Workroom charges	2,200
Cash discounts	6%

25. Set up a profit and loss statement, showing rupee amounts only, using the following figures:

Gross sales	₹ 1,27,000
Closing inventory, at cost	29,000

Opening inventory, at cost	33,000
Miscellaneous expenses	5,000
Customer returns	6,000
Purchases, at cost	60,000
Rent and utilities	23,000
Payroll	30,000
Transportation charges	1,700
Cash discounts	896
Advertising	6,000

1.11 ACTIVITY

1. The housewares department in a specialty store had net sales of ₹ 15,00,000. The direct expenses during the period under consideration were:

Buying salaries	₹ 1,25,000
Selling salaries	2,75,000
Advertising	90,000
Receiving & marking	15,000
Wrapping & packing	10,000

   The gross margin achieved during this time was 34.0%. After reviewing this performance, management decided that expenses must be reduced. The manager was given the choice of either reducing the advertising budget to a maximum of ₹ 50,000 or eliminating a salesperson which would reduce selling salaries by ₹ 50,000.

   Which plan of action would you choose? Why? Explore the two options mathematically, and then state your choice. Justify your decision. Discuss the impact your strategy will have on net profit.

2. Go to mall near to you, visit each and every department. See the plan how goods have been displayed. Draw construction plan for each department. Do you find any discrepancy in sales promotion? How these discrepancies can affect profit-write a note and discuss with your friends.
3. Discuss the concept of customer returns and allowances with a retail shop owner, why are required.
4. Interview a FMCG distributor in your area, attempt to find out the distributor margin for 20 products.
5. Go to retail shop and watch for one day how salesmen attend the customers, write a report.

CHAPTER 2

Retail Pricing and Re-pricing

2.1 LEARNING OBJECTIVES

After reading this chapter you will learn

1. Concept of price in retails and price lines
2. How to structure individual prices and prices for a line?
3. Benefits of price line
4. Markup pricing
5. Re-pricing and Markdown pricing
6. How pricing helps to increase sales and profit?

2.2 RETAIL PRICING

Price in business is the result of an exchange and from that trade we assign a numerical monetary value to a good, service or asset. If Ram trades Shyam 4 apples for an orange, the price of an orange is 4 apples. Inversely, the price of an apple is 1/4 oranges.

Price is only part of the information we get from observing an exchange. The other part is the volume of the goods traded per unit time, called the rate of purchase or sale. From this additional information we understand the extent of the market and the elasticity of the demand and supply.

The concept of price is central to microeconomics where it is one of the most important variables in resource allocation theory (also called price theory). Price is also central to marketing where it is one of the four variables in the marketing mix that business people use to develop a marketing plan.

In general terms price is the result of an exchange or transaction that takes place between two parties and refers to what must be given up by one party (i.e., buyer) in order to obtain something offered by another party (i.e., seller).

Price is commonly confused with the notion of cost as in "I paid a high cost for buying my new plasma television". Technically, though, these are different concepts. Price is what a buyer pays to acquire products from a seller. Cost concerns the seller's investment (e.g., manufacturing expense) in the product being exchanged with a buyer. For marketing organizations seeking to make a profit the hope is that price will exceed cost so the organization can see financial gain from the transaction. Finally, while product pricing is a main topic for discussion when a company is examining its overall profitability, pricing decisions are not limited to forprofit companies. Not-for-profit organizations, such as charities, educational institutions and industry trade groups, also set prices, though it is often not as apparent. For instance, charities seeking to raise money may set different "target" levels for donations that reward donors with increases in status (e.g., name in newsletter), gifts or other benefits. While a charitable organization may not call it a price in their promotional material, in reality these donations are equivalent to price setting since donors are required to give a contribution in order to obtain something of value

Price is a strong motivation in consumer buying habits. It is a competitive weapon and, very frequently, it is the only way to attract customer patronage when merchandise assortments are comparable, if not identical. Because many factors influence pricing, it can be considered an art as well as a science.

In large industrial organizations, the actual pricing decisions are generally the responsibility of management. In large retail stores, the actual pricing of merchandise is determined by individual departmental buyers or a comparable person designated by the particular organizational structure. Top management, however, does formulate the basic price policies of the store, such as the implementation of a policy of underselling the competition by 1096 on all items. Although the retailer establishes the price of individual items as they are offered for sale, ultimately, the total of all purchases must realize maximum profits. In the final analysis, the volume of sales as an aggregate figure must be great enough to cover not only the costs of merchandise sold, but also to provide a profit. Pricing, therefore, is an integral part of merchandising that requires training and skill.

Pricing refers to price lining, which is the practice of predetermining the retail prices at which an assortment of merchandise will be carried. A retail buyer selects and offers a merchandise assortment to the consumer at a specific price point, or price line, such as ₹ 15, ₹ 20, and so on.

2.3 THE STRUCTURING OF PRICE LINES

A buyer creates a stock assortment by considering what price lines to carry and the depth of assortment offered at the various price points. The number of price lines, and those particular price lines in the assortments, can help reflect the desired character that management wishes to project. The emphasis of a stock by price lines depends on the composition of the consumer segment that management wishes to attract. Usually, there is a price structure around which buying for a specific retail establishment is concentrated. For example, the sportswear department stocks tops to retail for ₹ 25; this price line may cover a variety of types, fabrics, and sizes. The buyer, with the proper source of information, knows that this particular store's customers will pay ₹ 25 for a top.

The sportswear department, however, may stock a variety of tops that retail from ₹ 8 to ₹ 40. This is called the price range, which refers to the spread from the lowest to the highest price line carried. Most customers generally prefer to concentrate their purchases at either one price line or several that are relatively close to each other. Price zone refers to a series of price lines that are likely to appeal to one group of the store's customers. When more than two price lines are stocked, a price zone situation exists. The price zones can be referred to as

- Volume price zone,
- Promotional price zone, and
- Prestige price zone.

Generally, the promotional price zone refers to the lower price lines carried; the volume price zone is the middle price lines where the largest percentage of sales occur; and the prestige price zone refers to the highest price lines carried in a department, which "tone up" the assortment. This distribution curve typically occurs within a price range, regardless of the price lines

For instance, a T-shirt can have three ranges 100 to 120 rupees (volume price zone), 120 to 200 rupees (promotional price zone) or 200 to 500 rupees (Prestige price zone).

2.3.1 Setting Individual Retail Prices and/or Price lines

The pricing of individual items and the establishment of price lines require experience and skill. When pricing merchandise as it is bought, a buyer must always consider its saleability in terms of its retail price, remembering that the aggregate of all prices must be high enough to cover merchandise costs, operating expenses, a fair profit return, possible reductions, shortages, and discounts to employees. Variations in pricing occur because there are some non-controllable factors that influence pricing decisions, such as the volatility of ready-to-wear. Because they influence the setting of the retail price, the basic factors to consider in pricing are:

- Wholesale costs.
- Competition.
- Price maintenance policies of manufacturers, such as "suggested" retail prices.
- Handling and selling costs.
- Store policies, such as "off-price" policy
- Nature of the goods, such as markdown risk in fashion goods.

- Correlation among departments.
- Supply and demand factors.

2.3.2 Advantages of Price Linings

The practice of offering merchandise for sale at a limited number of predetermined price points creates several merchandising problems, but the practice is prevalent because the advantages are numerous and significant. The advantages of price lining are that it:

- Simplifies customer choice, which facilitates selling.
- Enables the store to offer wide assortments at bestselling price lines.
- Simplifies buying by limiting the range of wholesale costs.
- Reduces the size of stock, resulting in more favourable stock turnover and decreased markdowns.
- Simplifies stock control.
- Decreases marking costs.
- Provides a basis for stock/sales control of customer preferences by price.

2.4 MARK-UP PRICING

Merchandising, or the act of buying and selling, is performed by the retailer, who selects and buys merchandise that is offered for resale to the consumer. To make a profit, the retail merchandiser must set the proper price on the merchandise. Although the profitable pricing of selected individual items cannot always be done by applying a mathematical formula, the three basic elements involved in the pricing of all goods are the cost of the merchandise, the retail price, and the difference between them, which is referred to as markup (MU). **Markup** is the amount that is added to the cost price of merchandise to arrive at a retail price. This amount must be large enough to cover the cost of the merchandise, the expenses incurred to sell it, and the desired profit. The aim of proper pricing can be expressed by the following:

Cost of goods + Markup = **Retail price**

2.4.1 Calculating Markup Percentage on Cost

What is the markup percentage on cost, when the markup is ₹ 8 and the cost is ₹ 10?

MU% = ₹ 8 (Markup)/₹ 10 (Cost)

If one knows any two of the basic pricing factors, the third can be calculated both in amounts and/or in percentage relationships. The following formulas show the relationship

Retail = Cost + rupee markup.

2.4.1.1 Solved Example

A retailer buys a top for ₹ 100 and has a markup of ₹ 60. What is the retail price?

Solution:

Cost = ₹ 100

+ Markup = + 60

Retail price = ₹ 160

Although retailers pay for and sell merchandise in rupees, knowing the relationship of the three basic pricing elements (i.e., retail, cost, markup) in percentages and rupees is useful to the merchandiser. Frequently, the retailer thinks in terms of amount only, as for example, "My customers prefer a toy that retail for ₹ 18 to ₹ 25," or a resource quotes the cost of an item to a retailer at ₹ 10 each. At other times, the retailer is concerned about achieving a 44.4% markup on an item that retails for ₹ 18 and costs ₹ 10. If this markup per cent is perceived as low, it may determine whether a particular item will be purchased. At still another time, the buyer thinks simultaneously in terms of rupees and percentages. For example, in determining the cost of an article to be purchased, a buyer must balance the retail price the customer is willing to pay with the particular markup percentage required by management.

2.4.1.2 Solved Example

What is the cost percentage and the markup percentage of a top that costs ₹ 10 and retails for ₹ 18?

Costs % = ₹ 10 (Cost)/₹ 18 (Retail) = 55.6% = ₹ 8 Markup (₹ 18 – ₹ 10)

Retail % = 100

Costs % = 55.6%

Martup = 44.4%

The markup percentage is commonly called the cost complement.

Solution:

Markup % = 80%

Generally, the retail calculation of markup is more acceptable because retailers also figure expenses and profits as a percentage of retail sales. Thus, they tend to consider price lines, stocks, and customer demands in retail values when making plans, and the calculation of markup on retail price is consistent with this approach.

The retailer faces numerous purchase planning and merchandise pricing problems when buying goods for resale. To achieve maximum profits, the same estimated initial (original) markup percentage is not applied to all purchases. The astute merchandiser sets an ultimate goal, but realizes that unexpected situations may cause deviations as goods are sold to individual purchasers. Therefore, manipulation of the markup and sales volume ultimately will provide the largest possible profit. Calculations of the various buying and pricing situations that may occur in merchandising are expressed in formulas that must be understood by all retail merchandisers.

2.4.1.3 Solved Example

What is the markup per cent on an item that costs ₹ 6.50 and is priced at ₹ 12.75?

Solution:

Given: Retail = ₹ 12.75 – Cost = ₹ 6.50 Markup = 6.25

Markup % = 6.25/12.75*100 = 49%

When the individual cost and the individual retail do not change, but the number of purchased pieces varies, the markup percentage is the same whether it is calculated for one piece or for the entire quantity purchased. The following calculations illustrate this principle:

2.4.1.4 Solved Example

What is the markup percentage on a purchase of 12 pieces that cost ₹ 6.50 each and are retailed at ₹ 12.75 each?

Solution:

Total retail – Total cost = 153 – 78 = 75

Mark up% = 75/153*100 = 49

2.4.1.5 Solved Example

A buyer bought 150 handbags that cost ₹ 22.50 each. The buyer then retailed 50 pieces for ₹ 40 each, 75 pieces for ₹ 48 each, and the balance for ₹ 55 each. What is the markup percentage on this purchase?

Solution:

Total retail = 50*40 + 75*48 + 25*55 = ₹ 6,975

Total Cost = 150*22.50 = 3375

Markup = 3600

Markup % = 3600/6975*100 = 51.60%

2.4.1.6 Solved Example

A jewellery buyer has an unadvertised promotion on rings at a special price of ₹ 25 each. The group consists of 75 pieces that cost: 15 pieces @ ₹ 10.00 each 40 pieces @ ₹ 12.50 each 20 pieces @ ₹ 16.00 each

What is the markup per cent on this group?

Solution:

Total retail = 75 pieces × ₹ 25 = ₹ 1,875

Total cost= 15 pieces × ₹ 10.00 + 40 pieces × ₹ 12.50 + 20 pieces × ₹ 16.00 = 970

Rupee markup on entire group = ₹ 905

Total retail Markup % on entire purchase = 905/1875 = 48.3%

2.4.1.7 Solved Example

A manufacturer quotes a cost of ₹ 42 per dozen for a visor; the markup that he wants is 51.7%. At what retail price should the item be marked to obtain the desired markup?

Solution:

Cost per piece = 42/12 = ₹ 3.50

Retail = Cost/(100 – markup%)

Cost *100/(100 – Markup) = 3.50 /(100 – 51.7)% = 3.50/0.483 = ₹ 7.25

2.4.1.8 Solved Example

A children's underwear buyer plans to retail pajamas for ₹ 10.95 with a 48% markup. What is the maximum price the buyer can pay for the pajamas to be sold at this price line?

Solution:

Given: Retail = ₹ 10.95

Cost = Retail × (100% – Markup %)

Cost = ₹ 10.95 (Retail) × (100% – 48%)

= ₹ 10.95 × 52% (Cost complement %)

Cost = ₹ 5.69

2.5 RE-PRICING OF MERCHANDISING

The dynamic nature of merchandising makes the repricing of goods in retailing universal. Price adjustments are made to either increase or decrease the original retail price placed on merchandise. These changes in prices must be properly recorded to:

- Achieve an accurate book inventory figure used in the retail method of inventory.
- Plan initial (original) markup goals when pricing goods.
- Control and manage the amount received in an attempt to merchandise at a profit.

The repricing of goods for sale is constant, the causes are numerous, and the skill required is considerable. It is rare that a retailer makes an upward adjustment to the retail price, and often a buyer is forced to make a downward retail price change on a significant portion of sales. In a profit and loss statement the downward differences frequently have a group heading of retail reductions that include:

- Markdowns.
- Employee discounts.
- Shortages.

Although all retail reductions have an impact on markup, they are, for the most part, considered a necessity. Their study is of major importance, for only with complete understanding of their use can the retailer turn them into a dynamic and advantageous merchandising tool.

2.6 MARKDOWNS

The most common and important type of price adjustment is technically called markdown (MD). It is the lowering or reducing of the original or previous retail price on one item or a group of items. For example, a toy that was retailed for ₹ 25 when it was received in the store was reduced to ₹ 18 because it became soiled. This price adjustment is called a markdown because the retail value of the merchandise was lowered. The difference between the new selling price (₹ 18) and the former price (₹ 25) is ₹ 7. The amount by which the retail value has been lowered is called the markdown and is the meaningful figure to the merchandiser. The merchandiser expresses markdowns as a percentage of net sales of all goods during a period, month, or year. Frequently, the merchandiser needs to calculate the markdown percentage that is necessary to sell a group of items. When this occurs, the markdown is still expressed as a percentage of the net sales figure.

2.6.1 The Purpose of Markdowns

Markdowns are "a cure, not a curse." This merchandising tool can be used to good advantage if the retailer realizes the objectives of markdowns. The major aims of reductions are:

- To stimulate the sale of merchandise to which customers are not responding satisfactorily
- To attract customers to stores by offering "bargains."
- To meet competitive prices.
- To provide open-to-buy money to purchase new merchandise.
- To create special "promotions," or sales (e.g., Birthday sales).

2.6.2 Causes of Markdowns

By analyzing all the possible causes of markdowns, a merchandiser can make an effort to minimize them. The most common causes (not in order of importance) are listed below:

- Buying errors, which include: Overbuying in quantities.
- Buying of wrong sizes.
- Buying of poor styles, quality, materials, and colors.
- Poor timing in ordering goods. Receiving and accepting merchandise that has been shipped late.
- Pricing errors, which include: Poor timing of markdowns. Setting the initial price too high. Not being competitive in price for same goods. Deferring markdowns too long. Calculated risks of carrying "prestige" merchandise.
- Selling errors, which include: Poor stock-keeping.
- Careless handling that results in soiled and damaged goods. Failure to display merchandise properly or advantageously. Uninformed salespeople.
- Special sales from stock, which include: Off-price promotions. Multiple sales (e.g., 3 for ₹ 100).
- Broken assortments, remnants, and so on.
- Necessary price adjustments.
- Remainders from special sales.

2.6.3 Timing of Markdowns

Accurate timing of markdowns can help reduce the amount of the markdown needed to sell the merchandise. It is suggested that merchandise be analyzed and reduced when:

- Merchandise becomes "slow selling."
- The customer demand is sufficient to sell the merchandise with a minimum price reduction.
- The consumer's interest in the merchandise in stock may diminish because of the appearance of a new fashion or product, or of a lower price.

2.6.4 The Amount of the Markdown

Judgment is required to determine the price at which items can be cleared quickly. The pricing of goods is a major factor in the control of markdowns. It is difficult to generalize on the amount of the markdown to be taken because the "right" price depends on:

- The reasons for the reduction.
- The nature of the merchandise.
- The time of the selling season (the proper moment during the selling season).
- The quantity on hand.
- The original (initial) markup.

Because the purpose of a markdown is to sell the merchandise quickly, the size of the markdown must be large enough to produce the desired results. Some rules to be considered in repricing are:

- The first markdown should be sharp enough to move a considerable amount of the goods.
- The markdown should be sufficiently large to attract customers who rejected the merchandise at its original price.
- The price may be reduced sufficiently to appeal to the next price zone customer.
- Markdowns should not be so large as to invite customer suspicion.
- Small markdowns are ineffective.
- Small, successive markdowns may increase the total loss.

2.6.5 Markdown Calculations

To find the amount of markdown taken when there is a group of items, it is customary to first determine the difference per piece between the present and new retail prices, and then to determine the total cost of the markdown.

Rupee markdown = Original retail price – New retail price

2.6.5.1 Solved Example

A buyer reduces 93 calculators from ₹ 15 to ₹ 10. What is the total markdown in rupees?

Solution:

Original or present retail ₹ 15.00

New retail = 10.00

Rupee markdown = ₹ 5.00 per piece

Total Rupee Markdown = 93 pieces × ₹ 5.00 = ₹ 465

However, the retailer frequently advertises markdowns as a percentage off the current retail price; for example, "25% off the selling price."

Rupee markdown = Percentage off × Present retail price

2.6.5.2 Solved Example

A store advertises 25% off on a group of 50 chairs currently retailed at ₹ 100 each. What is the total rupee markdown?

Solution:

Percentage off markdown

= 25% × 100

Retail = 25 = 50 pieces × 25

Total Rupee Markdown = ₹ 1,250

Even with the markdown, not all merchandise will sell. Therefore, after a reasonable period of time, an additional reduction must be made to move the remaining goods of that style and/or group.

Total markdown = First total rupee markdown + Second total rupee markdown

2.6.5.3 Solved Example

The men's clothing buyer had a group of 50 jackets priced at ₹ 225 each that were selling very slowly. To stimulate sales of these jackets, the buyer reduced the price of jackets in that group to ₹ 175. At this price, 40 pieces were sold in a short time. At a later date, the remaining pieces became shop-worn and needed a further reduction to clear them from stock. The buyer reduced them to ₹ 100 each and at that price they all sold out. What was the total rupee markdown taken?

Solution:

First Markdown on Group

Original retail price = ₹ 225

– First markdown price – 175

Amount of markdown per piece = ₹ 50

× Number of jackets = × 50

Total Markdown = ₹ 2,500

Second Markdown on Group

First markdown price – Second markdown price = 175 – 100

Amount of markdown per piece = 75

Second rupee markdown = 75*10 = 750

Total Markdown = 2500 + 750 = 3,250 rupees.

Markdowns taken are expressed as a percentage of the net sales for an accounting period. It is important to control and plan markdowns within a store. Markdown percentages can be calculated for an entire department, as shown in the following calculations:

Markdown % = Markdown/Net sales

2.6.5.4 Solved Example

In March, Department ABC had net sales of ₹ 5,000. The markdowns taken for March totalled ₹ 500. What was the markdown percentage for March?

Solution:

Markdown % = ₹ 500 Markdown/₹ 5,000 Net Sales = 10%

Markdown percentages can be used to evaluate a group of items and/or a vendor. The following shows this type of calculation:

Markdown % = MD/Total rupee sales of group's final selling prices

2.6.5.5 Solved Example

A buyer had a special selling price group of 100 plastic belts marked at ₹ 16 each. At the end of the season, the 15 pieces that were unsold were reduced to ₹ 10 each and sold out immediately. What is the markdown % on this purchase?

Solution:

Step 1: Determine markdown per piece. ₹ 16 to ₹ 10 = ₹ 6 each

Step 2: Determine markdown amount.

15 pieces reduced = 15 pieces × ₹ 6 = ₹ 90 Markdown

Step 3: Determine final selling price sales of group. 85 pcs × ₹ 16 = ₹ 1,360

15 pcs × ₹ 10 = + 150

Sales of group = ₹ 1,510 Markdown % = 90/1,510

Sales of group Markdown % = 5.96% or 6%

2.6.6 Calculating Markdown Cancellations

It is easier to describe a markdown cancellation than to define it. When the markdown price is raised to a higher retail price, it is considered a cancellation of a markdown. Cancellations may occur after special sales from stock, if the remaining merchandise is repriced upward. The restoration of a markdown price to the former retail is a markdown cancellation.

Currently, markdown cancellations are much less common because most large stores electronically program temporary markdowns into the cash register. This means of recording the markdown as the reduced offering when an item is being sold is called a point-of-sale (POS) markdown. It eliminates the need to mark the goods with the reduced price, and, subsequently, to remark the goods to the original price.

Markdown cancellation = Higher retail – Markdown price

2.6.6.1 Solved Example

After a one-day sale, a buyer marked up the remaining 12 pieces to the original price of ₹ 50, which had been reduced to ₹ 43 for the special event. What was the amount of the markdown cancellation?

Solution:

Markdown cancellation

₹ 50 Higher retail – 43 Markdown price

17 Difference per piece 12 Pieces × ₹ 7 Difference

Markdown Cancellation = ₹ 84

2.6.6.2 Solved Example

A buyer reduces 75 pieces from ₹ 50 to ₹ 43 for a oneday sale. After the sale, the remaining 28 pieces were marked up to the original price and were sold out at that price.

(a) What was the gross markdown in rupees?

(b) What was the markdown cancellation?

(c) Find the net markdown in rupees.

Solution:

(a) Determine gross markdown.

Gross markdown = ₹ 50 – ₹ 43 = ₹ 7 per piece = 75 pcs. × ₹ 7 Markdown

Gross markdown = ₹ 525

(b) Determine markdown cancellation.

Markdown cancellation = ₹ 43 to ₹ 50 = ₹ 7 per piece

= 28 pcs. × ₹ 7 Markdown cancellation = ₹ 196

(c) Determine net markdown.

Gross markdown = ₹ 525 – Markdown cancellation = –196 = ₹ 329 (Net markdown)

2.7 EMPLOYEE DISCOUNTS

It is common practice for a retail store to give its employees a reduction off a retail price. This type of retail reduction is called an employee discount. As noted previously, this is another type of price adjustment that must be recorded because it lowers the value of merchandise. This reduction is generally stated as a percentage off the retail price (e.g., a 20% discount). It must be recorded by the statistical department of the accounting division for accuracy of the book inventory figure under the retail method of inventory. The cumulative amount of employees' discounts is usually shown on the profit and loss statement under the general heading of "retail reductions."

2.7.1 Solved Example

Store X grants its employees a 20% discount on all merchandise purchased. If a salesperson buys an item that retails for ₹ 16.95, what is the employee discount in rupees? What is the amount paid for the item?

Solution:

Retail price of item = ₹ 16.95

Discount allowed = 20%

Employee discount = 16.95 × 20% = 3.39

Employee's Price = 16.95 – 3.39 = 13.56

2.8 ADDITIONAL MARKUP

An additional markup is a type of price adjustment that raises the price of merchandise already in stock. It increases the original retail price placed on the merchandise. It is taken after and in addition to the original (initial) markup. Although it is not a common type of adjustment, a provision must be made when an upward change of the retail prices of existing inventories is necessary. For example, an upward change of wholesale costs might necessitate the immediate upward revision of retail prices on existing inventory.

2.9 MARKUP CANCELLATION

Markup cancellation is a downward price adjustment that offsets an original inflated markup to a markup that is more normal. It is used to adjust the markup on a purchase in accordance with the original intent and is not used to manipulate stock values. It is justified when quoting "comparable value" prices used in promoting goods. For example, a resource offers a retailer gloves at ₹ 7, which is lower than the normal cost of ₹ 10. This item may be presently in stock and retailing for ₹ 22. During the permitted time, the gloves costing ₹ 7, which originally retailed at ₹ 22, are reduced to ₹ 14. This lowered price appears to the public as a markdown, yet results in a markup that is close to normal. The ₹ 8 difference between ₹ 22 and ₹ 14 is the markup cancellation.

2.10 PRICE CHANGE PROCEDURES

An efficient system of reporting and recording price changes is important the following three reasons:

- Facilitation of the review of price adjustments.
- Accurate calculation of inventory records.
- Identification of shortages.

2.11 THE RELATIONSHIP OF REPRICING TO PROFIT

Every price change has an impact on gross margin and net profits. Because the elimination of price adjustments in retailing is impossible, stores must classify each type of adjustment separately so that they can be analyzed, planned, and controlled. Markdowns, the major type of price changes, reduce the retail price, causing a decrease in gross margin that is further reflected in a decrease and/or elimination of profit. With certain merchandise or classifications, the markdown risk is frequently anticipated. It is offset by planning a higher initial (original) markup. Unfortunately, profit cannot always be preplanned because there are business forces that do not permit easy solutions to problems (e.g., non-acceptance of a newly introduced fashion or style, change in competition, etc.). However, it is important for the retailer to *realize* the effect of price adjustments on gross margin and profit as illustrated by the following example

Initial retail value of new purchase ₹ 1,05,000 = 100.0%

Cost of goods sold – 49,980 = – 47.6%

Gross margin 55,020 = 52.4%

– Operating expenses – 45,990 = – 43.8%

Net profit ₹ 9,030 = 8.6%

The total retail reductions for the period are ₹ 5,000:

Net sales = 1,00,000 = 100.0%

– Cost of goods sold = – 49,980 = – 50.0%

Gross margin = 50,020 = 50.0%

Operating expenses – 45,990 = – 46.%

Net Profit = 4,030 = 4.0%

2.12 PROBLEMS FOR PRACTICE

1. Fill in the blank spaces for each of the exercises below. (Note: Several of the examples may be done without written calculations.)

	Retail	Cost	₹ MU	MU%
a.	₹ 5.00	₹ 2.70		
b.	₹ 14.95	₹ 7.50		
c.	₹ 200.00		₹ 90.00	
d.	₹ 1.75	₹ 9.60/doz.		
e.	₹ 29.95	₹ 14.50		
f.	₹ 10.00	₹ 60.00/doz.		
g		₹ 15.00 each		48%
h.		₹ 42.50 each		46.6%
i.		₹ 106.00/doz.		45%
j		₹ 15.00/doz.		47.5%
k.	₹ 100.00			49%
1.	₹ 80.00			50%
m		₹ 16.00	₹ 14.00	
n.		₹ 55.00	₹ 45.00	
o.	₹ 75.00			52%
p	₹ 3.98			37.8%
q-		₹ 21.60/doz.		46.5%
r.	₹ 9.95	₹ 72.00/doz.		
s.	₹ 465.00	₹ 235.00		
t.	₹ 590.00	₹ 310.00	₹ 280.00	

2. A buyer of men's furnishings paid ₹ 96 per dozen for wool blend knit neckties. If the desired markup was 58%, what was the exact retail per tie? What price line would the buyer probably use in ticketing the ties for the selling floor?

3. A buyer is interested in a group of tweed jackets costing ₹ 35 each. If the required markup is 53.6%, what would be the minimum retail price for each jacket? If the buyer had previously bought these jackets at ₹ 39.75 and retailed them for ₹ 79.50, what was this previous markup percentage?
4. For a holiday catalog, a buyer makes a special purchase of infant knit shirts that cost:
   - 40 dozen at ₹ 60/dozen.
   - 20 dozen at ₹ 72/dozen.
   - 18 dozen at ₹ 66/dozen.

   If the shirts all retail at the same unit price of ₹ 11, what markup percentage will be yielded?
5. A suit that costs ₹ 67.50 has a markup of 62.5%. What should be the retail price of each suit?
6. A buyer purchased 50 assorted leather attache cases that cost ₹ 79.50 each, and subsequently merchandised them as follows:
   - 25 pieces to retail for ₹ 175 each.
   - 10 pieces to retail for ₹ 150 each.
   - 15 pieces to retail for ₹ 125 each.

   Find the markup percentage on this purchase.
7. An outerwear buyer arranges a special purchase from a manufacturer who offers a group of 150 raincoats (with varying costs) at one low price of ₹ 25 each. The buyer decides to price this purchase as follows:
   - 50 pieces to retail at ₹ 35.95 each.
   - 50 pieces to retail at ₹ 45.00 each.
   - 50 pieces to retail at ₹ 55.00 each.

   What markup percentage is realized on this purchase?
8. Calculate the markup percentage on the following order placed by the handbag department:
   - $3^{1/2}$ dozen, costing ₹ 180 per dozen to retail for ₹ 32.50 each.
   - 15 pieces, costing ₹ 37.50 each to retail for ₹ 79 each.
9. The jewellery buyer wants to spend ₹ 15,000 at retail. The department maintains a 56.7% markup. The buyer needs a minimum of 600 pairs of earrings to cover each branch with an adequate assortment.

   (a) What should be the retail price per pair?

   (b) What should be the cost per pair?

10. The sportswear buyer wants to spend ₹ 84,000 at retail. Orders for ₹ 18,500, at cost, have already been placed. If the planned markup per cent to be achieved is 52.5%, how much, in rupees, does the buyer have left to spend at cost?
11. On Columbus Day, the suit buyer in Department 25 offered a "30% off" for an unadvertised special. On that special sale day, 50 suits, style #1,000, vendor #39, originally priced at ₹ 100 each were sold. Calculate the total rupee markdown taken. Record the markdown on this price change form.

(X) TO SHOW TYPE
- MARK-DOWN
- CANCELLATION OF MARK-DOWN
- MARK-UP

PRICE CHANGE

ISSUED AT: ☐ Paramus ☐ Danbury ☐ Hartford

DEPT NO. | PART 1 | B | CLASS | DATE

ISSUE SEPARATE SHEETS FOR MARK-DOWN, CANCELLATION MARK-UP STOLEN AND SALVAGE ITEMS

Show Reason By Letter		Item Description Vendor – Style – Name	Quantity	SEA LET	Verified Quantity	Old Retail	New Retail	Difference	Amount
A Promotional Purchase Remainders ____									
B Slow Moving Or Inactive Stock ____									
C Special Sales From Stock ____									
D Price Adjustments ____									
E Broken Assortments and Remnants ____									
F Shopworn Soiled or Damaged ____									
G Allowance to customer ____									
H Stolen ____									
J Salvage									

DO NOT ENTER ANY PRICE CHANGES BELOW THIS LINE

DEPT MGRS SIGNATURE DATE | MDSE VP OR MGRS SIGNATURE DATE | MARKERS SIGNATURE DATE | TOTAL DO NOT CARRY THIS TOTAL FORWARD

SEND PART 1 TO STATISTICAL PART 2 TO NEW YORK STORE DEPT MGR LEAVE PART 3 IN BOOK | FOR STATISTICAL DEPT USE ONLY

12. For the month of November, a suit buyer took markdowns totalling ₹ 1,600. During this month, the net sales for the department amounted to ₹ 50,000. What was the markdown percentage for this month?
13. In the month of July, a domestics buyer took markdowns totalling ₹ 1,800. During this month, the net sales for the department were ₹ 25,000. If the original markdown plan for this month called for 8% markdowns, was the actual markdown over or under the original plan, and by how much in rupees? What was the actual markdown percentage?
14. The seasonal plan for a shoe department shows sales of ₹ 1,53,000, with planned markdowns of 6.4%.

(a) What is the planned amount of markdowns?

(b) If the actual markdowns are ₹ 7,200, how does the real percentage compare with the plan? Is the actual percentage more or less than planned? By how much?

15. A buyer reduces 75 jackets from ₹ 39.50 to ₹ 32.95 for a sale. A short while after the sale, the remaining 30 jackets are reduced further to ₹ 27. At that price, they all sold out. Find the total markdown amount taken.

16. A coat department had sales of ₹ 60,000 for the month of November. During the month, the buyer reduced 50 coats from ₹ 60 to ₹ 40 and another 100 coats from ₹ 80 to ₹ 60.

(a) What was the total markdown for the month?

(b) Find the markdown percentage for the month.

17. A buyer had 400 pocket calculators in stock at ₹ 25 each. They were on sale for ₹ 18 each for a one day special event. At the end of the day, 210 remained unsold and were sold eventually at their original price.

(a) What was the total markdown in rupees?

(b) What was the markdown percentage on this purchase?

18. For Columbus Day, the buyer advertised all suede coats at 35% off. The records indicated sales of:

- 50 pieces with original retail of ₹ 275 each.
- 30 pieces with original retail of ₹ 195 each.
- 10 pieces with original retail of ₹ 150 each.

(a) What was the total markdown in rupees?

(b) If sales for October were planned at ₹ 80,270, with estimated markdowns of 9%, did the buyer have more markdown money to spend for the month? If so, how much? If not, why not?

2.13 ACTIVITY

1. At the end of October, a key resource offered a department store buyer a group of acrylic knit tops that are promotionally priced at ₹ 96 per dozen. The resource, who owns 60 dozen pieces, quoted this low price providing the purchaser bought the entire group. These tops are comparable in quality and styling to similar merchandise purchased from this vendor at ₹ 144 per dozen that sold well at ₹ 25 each earlier in the season with the normal department markup. The group now being offered by the resource consists of three different styles currently in demand. Group A has 30 dozen pieces, Group B consists of 20 dozen pieces, and Group C is 10 dozen pieces. As a combined offering, the sizes are well balanced and the colors are "fashion" for this season. Group A is a "staple" in styling, Group B reflects this season's "hot seller," and

Group C is considered "avant garde" in both color and silhouette. Because sales are sluggish, the buyer wants to stimulate selling for Election Day by retailing these tops with only a 50% markup. By taking a lower than normal markup, the buyer hopes this purchase will result in additional sales and be a total "sellout."

As the buyer reviews the stock condition of the department, it seems the inventory is higher than planned and the report shows that:

(a) 55% of the inventory is current and salable.

(b) 150 pieces remain from a recent promotion, currently priced at ₹ 19 each, and are broken in size and color.

(c) A group of 75 pieces, all one style, priced at ₹ 22.50 each, are selling very slowly.

(d) 15 pieces are badly soiled and are marked ₹ 25 each.

The buyer also noted that there is ₹ 1,000 of markdown money available in November.

The buyer feels the purchase would be ultimately advantageous because increased departmental activity will lead to improved sales. To assure this high volume day, the proper pricing of this purchase, plus an accurate count of the current inventory is essential.

To make the correct decisions, the following questions must be answered:

(a) If this group purchase were to be retailed at the normal markup, what would be the retail per piece? What degree of excitement would this produce by quoting a higher "comparable value?"

(b) Determine the markup percentage achieved if the three groups are retailed as follows:

- Group A at ₹ 16 each.
- Group B at ₹ 18 each.
- Group C at ₹ 20 each.

The last group seems to represent particularly good value.

(c) Should the available November markdown money (₹ 1,000) be used now to clear the present inventory, by reducing the three groups all to ₹ 16 and using their comparable value prices? Or should the buyer defer these reductions (which seem inevitable), until the storewide clearance in December?

Decide what course of action the buyer should pursue and mathematically justify your suggestions as you apply the principles in pricing and repricing.

2. Visit a retail shop, buy a product and ask for cash memo. Note down all the particulars mentioned in the receipt/cash memo. Write a note what a cash memo should have.

3. Go the store of your college. Ask the store incharge, how goods are ordered, documents he signs when he orders, documents he signs when goods are delivered to him, take a copy of delivery challan, bills, cash receipts. Now take a look at the registers he maintains. How entries are made for receipts and issues. Write a note of all documents and discuss in the class.

4. If in case of 3, it is computerised system, take a note what is manual and what is computerised and write a note in details

5. Go to a mall and find out 20 items which have markdown prices.

CHAPTER 3

Relationship of Markup to Profit

3.1 LEARNING OBJECTIVES

In this chapter you will learn

1. How to fix up prices of merchandise?
2. How these prices affect produce?
3. How to decrease prices in case of slow down

Markup, which is simply the difference between retail prices placed on merchandise and the cost of this merchandise, has an effect on:

- Sales volume it can generate.
- Markdowns it can cause.
- Gross margin it can achieve.
- Profits it can produce.

As a result, markup must be estimated, always controlled, and, if necessary, adjusted. Because basic markup calculations in both rupee s and percentages are used in buying decisions as they relate to a single item or a group of items, the buyer responsible for a particular department is involved with the markups planned and obtained. These markups are constantly monitored because the desired gross margin depends on how successfully they are achieved.

3.2 TYPES OF MARKUP

3.2.1 Initial Markup

Initial markup is the difference between the billed cost of merchandise and the original or first retail price placed on a given item or group of items. When freight charges are known, they are added to the billed cost when calculating initial markup. Certain vital factors and common practices must be considered in determining the initial markup; the following considerations cannot be ignored.

- Plan, in advance, an initial markup on merchandise when it is received in the store to ensure a favourable gross margin figure that will cover expenses and provide a reasonable profit.
- Forecast an initial markup percentage that will be required on all the merchandise handled during a particular period (i.e., a six month season), because it is virtually impossible to have available all the data necessary for the calculation of each purchase.
- Recognize that the gross margin figure can fluctuate because it is the result of many merchandising decisions.
- Understand that the initial markup placed on new purchases will be reduced by markdowns, shortages, and employee discounts.
- Be aware of and act on cash discounts offered to retailers in the purchase of goods, as well as estimated alteration costs.

For a department, an initial markup planned on a seasonal and/or annual basis can be expressed in either figures or percentages and usually is calculated for both. In most large retail stores, the buyer and/or divisional merchandise manager (under the guidance and supervision of the control division), establishes this initial markup as a guide to check against aggregate markups ob-tained in pricing new merchandise purchases. In addition, it is essential to know that the initial markup planned for a season must take into consideration the markups on the new purchases and the effect they have on the markup of the merchandise inherited from the last season, because the gross margin figure for the period depends on the markups achieved on all the inventory available for sale. Thus, in planning an initial markup, probable expenses, the profit goal, probable reductions, estimated alteration costs and anticipated sales must be projected first.

An initial markup is expressed as a percentage of the aggregate original retail price placed on the merchandise, not on the price at which the merchandise sold. The price at which the merchandise sold is expressed as sales plus reductions. For example, if sales are planned at ₹ 10,00,000 and all retail reductions at ₹ 1,50,000, the goods that eventually sell at ₹ 10,00,000 must be introduced into stock at ₹ 11,50,000 with the desired markup expressed as a percentage of this total.

3.2.2 Establishing an Initial Markup

To better appreciate the establishment of an initial markup, examine the methods commonly used to institute a seasonal markup, and the calculations (in both amount and percentages) as they appear in the chart and steps below.

3.2.2.1 Solved Example

Given	Amount	Percentage
Planned sales	10,00,000	100.0%
Estimated expenses	3,93,000	39.3%
Price reductions	1,50,000	15.0%
Profit	50,000	5.0%

Method:

1. Forecast the total sales for the season or the year (₹ 10,00,000).
2. Estimate the required expenses (₹ 3,93,000) and price reductions (₹ 1,50,000) needed to reach the sales plan.
3. Set a profit goal operating profit or department contribution (₹ 50,000).
4. Add the estimated expenses (₹ 3,93,000) to the price reductions (₹ 1,50,000) and profit (₹ 50,000) to determine the total markup (₹ 5,93,000).

   Total = Estimated expenses + Price reductions + Profit

   = 3,93,000 + 1,50,000 + 50,000

   = ₹ 5,93,000

   Markup = 59,300

   Markup% = 59.3%
5. Determine the original retail price (₹ 11,50,000) by adding the planned reductions (₹ 1,50,000) to the planned sales (₹ 10,00,000).

   Planned sales + Price reductions = 10,00,000 + 1,50,000

   Original retail price = 11,50,000 = 115.0%
6. Compute the markup percentage (51.6%) by dividing the total markup ₹ 5,93,000) found in step 4 by the original price (₹ 11,50,000).

   Initial Mark up = 5,93,000/11,50,000 = 51.6%

The formula for calculating an initial markup percentage on goods purchased shows the amount of markup necessary to achieve a desire profit. This markup should cover expenses, reductions, and profits. These projections can be based on past results or calculated mathematically on the basis of anticipated sales, reductions, and expenses.

The equation to determine an initial markup percentage can spell out each factor (i.e., expenses + profits + markdowns + stock shortages + employee discounts), or it can be simplified (i.e., expenses + profits = gross margin and markdowns + stock shortages + employee discounts = retail reductions).

Because gross margin and retail reduction figures are more significant in planning than the analysis of expenses, shortages, and other factors, the second, simplified equation is more often used.

Initial markup % = (Gross margin % + Retail Reductions %)/(100% (Sales) + Retail Reductions %)

3.2.2.2 Solved Example

A store has a gross margin of 42.3% (39.3% expenses + 3% profit) and retail reductions (markdowns, shortages, and employee discounts) of 15%. What is the initial markup percentage?

Solution:

Initial MU % = (42.3% + 15.0%)/(100% + 15%) = 57.3%/115.0% = 49.8%

3.2.2.3 Solved Example

A store plans sales of ₹ 10,00,000, retail reductions of ₹ 1,50,000, and requires a gross margin of ₹ 4,23,000 (i.e., expenses ₹ 3,93,000, profit ₹ 30,000). What should be the initial markup percentage?

Solution:

Initial MU % = (₹ 4,23,000 (GM) + 1,50,000 (Retail reductions))/(10,00,000 (Sales) + ₹ 1,50,000 (Retail reductions)

= 5,73,000/11,50,000 = 49.8%

3.2.3 Cumulative Markup

Cumulative markup is the markup percentage achieved on all goods available for sale from the beginning of a given period. It is an average markup because it is the markup percentage obtained on the accumulated inventory at the beginning of the given period, plus the markup of all the new purchases received season to date. The cumulative markup in rupees equals the difference between the invoiced cost of the merchandise (including transportation) before cash discounts have been adjusted and the cumulative original retail prices of all merchandise handled (opening inventory + net purchases) during a given period of time. Markdowns do not enter into the calculation of the cumulative markup percentage.

Cumulative markup per cent = Cumulative markup rupees/cumulative retail amount.

3.2.3.1 Solved Example

On February 1, a department has an opening inventory of ₹ 2,00,000 at retail with markup of 49.0%. On July 31, the new purchases season to date amounted to ₹ 13,50,000 at retail with a 49.9% markup. Find the cumulative markup percentage achieved.

Solution:

Given information is in bold, and the other items are calculated from the basic markup formulas; each calculation is identified with the steps of the procedure.

	Cost	Retail	MU%
Opening inventory	1,02,000	2,00,000	49.0%
+ Purchases STD	+ 6,76,350	+ 13,50,000	49.9%
Total merchandise handled	7,78,350	₹ 15,50,000	49.8%

Step 1: Find the cost value of the retail opening inventory.

C = R × (100% – MU%)

C = 2,00,000 (100% – 49.0%)

C = 2,00,000 × 51%

C = ₹ 1,02,000

Step 2: Find the total cost value of all purchases season to date.

C = R × (100% = MU%)

C = 13,50,000 (100% – 49.9%)

C = 13,50,000 × 50.1%

C = 6,76,350

Step 3: Find the total retail value of total merchandise handled. ₹ 2,00,000 + 13,50,000 = 15,50,000

Step 4: Find the total cost value of total merchandise handled. ₹ 1,02,000 + 6,76,350 = 7,78,350

Step 5: Find the cumulative markup on total merchandise handled.

15,50,000 Cumulative retail – 7,78,350 = 7,71,650 Cumulative cost

Cumulative markup % = 7,71,650/15,50,000 = 49.8%

The new purchases required a 49.9% markup to achieve a 49.8% cumulative markup, because the merchandise of the opening inventory came into the period with only a 49% markup.

At this point, it must be understood that both the intial and cumulative markup are on merchandise purchased. Initial markup percentage refers to those markups obtained when pricing new merchandise purchases. Cumulative markup percentage is the amount of markup on all the merchandise available for sale, whether it is new purchases or stock on hand at the beginning of the period. The cumulative markup percentage is the initial markup percentage calculated from the beginning of the season to any given later date (e.g., the end of the season or year).

3.2.4 Maintained Markup

Before maintained markup is explained, it is essential to know that although gross margin and a maintained markup are related, they are not identical. Gross margin is the difference between net sales and the cost of merchandise sold, adjusted by subtracting cash discounts and adding alteration/workroom costs (i.e., total cost of merchandise sold). **Maintained Markup** (MMU) is the difference between net sales and the cost of merchandise sold without the credits of cash discounts and without adding alteration/workroom costs (i.e., gross cost of merchandise sold). If these differences are not considered in calculations, the gross margin and maintained markup figures will be the same. For both, the net sales figure reflects the final selling prices received for the goods sold, and the margin actually realized when the goods are sold. They are both markup on sales. The relationship between gross margin and maintained markup is revealed clearly in the following example:

Net sales =	₹ 10,00,000
Cost of goods sold	– 2,20,000
New purchases	+ 6,45,000
+ Inward freight	+ 14,000
Total merchandise handled	8,79,000
– Closing inventory	– 2,80,000
Gross cost of merchandise =	5,99,000
– Cash discounts earned =	– 32,000
Net cost of merchandise sold =	5,67,000
+ Alteration/workroom costs =	+ 10,000
Total cost of merchandise sold	– 5,77,000
Gross margin	4,23,000

GM = Net sales – Total cost of goods sold

= 10,00,000 (Sales) – 5,77,000 (Total cost of goods sold)

GM % = 4,23,000 Gross margin/10,00,000 Net sales = 42.3%

MMU % = Net sales – Gross cost of goods sold

= 10,00,000 Net sales – ₹ 5,99,000 (Gross cost of goods) = 4,01,000 Maintained margin/ 10,00,000

Net sales MMU % = 40.1%

3.2.4.1 Solved Example

A department planned an initial markup of 49.8% and retail reductions of 15%. What is the maintained markup?

Solution:

MMMU% = 49.8% – 15% × (100% – 49.8)

= 49.8% – 15% × 50.2%

= 49.8% – 7.53%

MMU % = 42.27 or 42.3%

Maintained markup is the markup actually achieved on the sale of the merchandise and is generally calculated for a department or, when desired, for a vendor analysis, which is an investigation of the profitability of each vendor's products sold by a retailer. It is not customary to plan a maintained markup, because it is the result of merchandising activities. The initial markup must be planned in advance so that the desired final or maintained markup goal is achieved. In addition, maintained markup must be large enough to cover expenses and provide a profit while, as previously explained, the initial markup must be high enough to anticipate and also cover all possible retail reductions (i.e., markdowns, shortages and employee discounts). However, once the initial markup and retail reductions are planned, the probable maintained markup can be projected.

3.3 BALANCING MARKUP

In the actual pricing of goods in retailing, it is seldom possible to obtain the same markup on all lines of merchandise, all classifications, all price lines, or all items carried within a particular department. In the real world of retailing, deviations from the planned seasonal markup will occur. These differences can be the result of competition, variations in special promotional merchandise offered by resources, special buying arrangements, private brands, imports, and other factors that rely on the buyer's judgment. Thus, to realize the planned markup necessary for a profitable operation, below average markups should be balanced by above average markups.

Averaging markups means adjusting the proportions of goods purchased at different markups, to achieve the desired aggregate markup, either for an individual purchase or for a certain period. In merchandising the purchases, the buyer builds a "cushion" or lowers the markup depending on the situation. This practice is prevalent in the fashion and fashion related industries.

There are diverse pricing policies that are determined by an industry or by the specific retailer. Some of these factors are odd pricing (i.e., ₹ 89.99 instead of ₹ 90); multiple unit pricing (i.e., one for ₹ 3.25, two for ₹ 6); loss leaders, when the item is sold below the retailer's cost; high low pricing, using high everyday prices combined with "specials" or low leader pricing on featured items advertised weekly. Each retailer must evaluate the usefulness of each type of pricing service. The appropriate cumulative markup originates from effective averaging of many purchases.

When solving problems that illustrate how markups are averaged or balanced, it is helpful to remember that:

- On a day-to-day basis, buyers strive to achieve a projected markup by the averaging process.
- Appropriate cumulative markups result from the effective averaging of many purchases, and the effects of this averaging on the entire inventory.
- Basic markup equations are applied to given information for calculation of the figures required for solutions.
- Solutions can be calculated readily when: It is understood what information is missing. The given information is determined. The calculations required for the solution (based on the given information) are identified.

3.3.1 Solved Example

For a special sale, a men's sportswear buyer plans to promote a ₹ 25 vest. Consequently, the buyer purchases 500 vests, and wants to achieve a 52% markup. An order for 100 vests that cost ₹ 10.75 each is also placed by this same buyer. What will be the average cost of the remaining pieces?

Solution:

Step 1: Find the total planned retail. 500 pieces × ₹ 25 = ₹ 12,500

Step 2: Find the total cost of total planned retail using a planned MU percentage.

$$C = R \times (100\% - MU\%)$$

$$C = 12{,}500 \times (100\% - 52\%)$$

$$C = 12{,}500 \times 48\%$$

$$C = 6{,}000$$

Step 3: Find the cost of purchases to date. 100 pieces × 10.75 = 1,075

Step 4: Find purchase balance in units and rupees.

Purchase balance = Total planned figures – Purchases to date.

(500 pieces cost 6,000) – (100 pieces cost 1,075) = (400 pieces cost 4,925)

Step 5: Find the average cost of purchase balance. Average cost of purchase balance = Cost on balance of purchase/Purchase balance number of units

= 4,925/400 pcs. = ₹ 12.31

In merchandising, a buyer must be able to manipulate markups, because purchases may be made that have two or more costs, and the buyer may want to determine an **average retail** that will achieve the desired markup percentage. Furthermore, the buyer may make purchases that have not only two or more costs, but may also have two or more retails. These situations require the proper proportion of varying retails to achieve the planned markup percentage because a buyer is always concerned with the aggregate results.

3.3.2 Solved Example

At the end of the season, a swimwear manufacturer offered a retailer 50 two-piece solid-color suits that cost ₹ 16.75 each, 75 nylon tank suits that cost ₹ 12.75 each, and 40 one-piece skirted suits that cost ₹ 14.75 each. The average retail price on each unit was based on the buyer's goal of obtaining a 49% markup on this purchase. What would be the average retail price of each swimsuit?

Solution:

Step 1: Find the total cost and total units of purchase.

50 suits @ 16.75 = 837.50

75 suits @ 12.75 = 956.25

40 suits @ 14.75 = 590.00

165 suits = 2,383.75

Step 2: Find the total retail from the planned MU percentage. R = Cost/(100% – 49%)

R = 2,383.75/51% R = 4,674.02

Step 3: Find average retail for each piece.

Average retail = Total retail/Total units purchased

= 4,674.02/165 pcs.

= ₹ 28.33

3.3.3 Solved Example

A coat buyer plans to buy ₹ 5,000 (retail) worth of merchandise. This same buyer requires a 49% MU. The first purchase is 50 coats costing ₹ 31.75, with a planned retail of ₹ 55. What MU percentage should the buyer obtain on the balance to attain the planned MU goal of 49%?

Step 1: Find the total cost of total planned retail from planned MU96.

C = R × (100% – MU%)

C = 5,000 × (100% – 49%)

C = 5,000 × 51%

C = 2,550

Step 2: Find the total cost and retail of purchases to date. 50 suits @ 31.75 = ₹ 1,587.50

Total cost 50 suits @ 55.00 = ₹ 2,750 Total retail

Step 3: Find purchase balance at cost and at retail.

Purchase balance = Total planned cost and retail amounts – Respective figures of purchases to date.

2,550 – 1,587.50 = ₹ 962.50

₹ 5,000 – ₹ 2,750 = ₹ 2,250

Step 4: Find the MU% on purchase balance. ₹ MU = R. – C.

MU = 2,250 – 962.50

MU = 1,287.50

MU % = MU/R

MU % = 1,287.50/2,250

MU % = 57.2%

Limitations of Markup

In the calculation of all types of markup, the focal point is generally on the markup percentage because it is particularly meaningful for analysis and comparison. However, under certain conditions, attention must be given to the total markup. Expenses are paid in rupees and profit is invested, reinvested, or taken to the bank in rupees. During periods of declining sales, a markup percentage initially deemed appropriate, may be insufficient for a profit because a certain markup percentage is based on a specific estimated sales figure. There is a correlation between these two figures.

For example, a buyer achieves sales of ₹ 3,00,000 and attains the required initial markup of 52% that would be large enough to cover expenses of 11,36,000 and markdowns of ₹ 12,000, and allow a profit of ₹ 8,000. In rupees and percentages this calculation would be:

Sales ₹ 30,000 (100%)

– Cost ₹ 1,44,00 (48%)

Initial Markup = ₹ 1,56,000 (52%)

Expenses (1,36,000 + 12,000)

₹ 1,48,000 (49.3%)

Total Profit ₹ 8,000 (2.7%)

If sales declined 10% to ₹ 2,70,000, the 52% markup may not yield a profit. As sales decline, the fixed nature of expenses will not decline proportionately to the sales, if at all, and it is not always possible to lower markdown reductions, which may increase to stimulate lagging sales. This type of situation can result in a loss despite the establishment of what seemed a satisfactory markup percentage. Students should calculate themselves.

Conversely, as sales increase, the markup percentage can decline even though the rupees markup is maintained at an adequate level. The astute retailer recognizes that the markup figure cannot be ignored while attempting to achieve a fixed markup percentage.

3.4 PROBLEMS FOR PRACTICE

1. A lingerie buyer determines that the department has net sales of 17,50,000, expenses of 3,15,000, and total reduction of 75,000. This buyer also wants to attain a net contribution of 4.5%. Find the initial markup percentage.
2. A department shows a gross margin of 41% (37.9% expenses + 3.1% profit) and lists retail reductions (i.e., markdowns, shortages, and employee discounts) of 13%. What is the initial markup percentage?
3. A chain of specialty shops plans sales of ₹ 15,00,000 and retail reductions of ₹ 2,60,000. It needs a gross margin of ₹ 6,05,000 (i.e., expenses ₹ 5,50,000, profit ₹ 55,000). What should be the initial markup percentage?
4. In a small leather goods department, the markdowns, including employee discounts, were 18.7%, stock shortage was 3.8%, and the gross margin was 46.6%. Determine the initial markup percentage.
5. A retailer in a boutique jewelry store has estimated expenses of 39%, markdowns at 15%, and stock shortage at 6.3%. A profit of 4% is desired. Calculate the initial markup percentage required.

6. The intimate apparel buyer wants to determine an initial markup percentage for the robe classification. The buyer knows that the gross margin is 44.0%, markdowns are at 31.4%, and shortages are at 0.6%. Calculate the initial markup percentage.
7. A buyer plans, for the period, net sales of ₹ 15,00,000 with a 49% gross margin. The acceptable markdowns are 12%, with employee discounts at 1%, and planned shortages of 2.5%. Cash discounts to be earned are estimated at 6%, and alteration costs are 0.5%. What initial markup percentage is needed to achieve the desired results?
8. Determine the initial markup percentage from the following data:

   Gross margin = 46.8%

   Markdowns = 10.0%

   Employee discounts = 1.5%

   Cash discounts to be earned = 5.0%

   Alteration costs = 0.5%
9. A hosiery buyer has an opening stock figure of ₹ 1,80,000, at retail, which carries a 52% markup. On March 31, new purchases since the start of the period were ₹ 9,90,000 at retail, carrying a 54% markup. Find the cumulative markup percentage on merchandise handled in this department to date.
10. The slipper department showed an opening inventory of ₹ 80,000 at retail with a markup of 48%. The purchases for that month amounted to ₹ 30,000 at cost, which were marked in at 52%. The initial markup planned for this department was 50.5%.

    (a) Determine the season to date cumulative markup percentage for the department.

    (b) Was the department markup achieved on target? If not, what factors caused a deviation?
11. A men's shop with an initial markup of 53% had markdowns of 12%, employee discounts of 2.5%, and shortages of 1.5%. What was the maintained markup percentage?
12. A sporting goods store has an initial markup of 44.5%. The expenses are 31%, markdowns are 12%, cost of assembling bicycles, etc. (i.e., workroom costs), are 6%, and shortages are 1%. What was the maintained markup percentage?
13. A buyer who needs ₹ 10,000 worth of merchandise at retail for a housewares department has written orders for ₹ 2,875.50 at cost. The planned departmental MU percentage is 53.5%. How much (in rupees) is left to spend at cost?
14. A December promotion of 1,500 crystal bud vases to retail at ₹ 40 each is planned. The buyer requires a 48.5% average markup and has made an initial purchase consisting of 1,200 units costing ₹ 23 each. What is the cost to be paid on each remaining unit? Comment on the buyer's "predicament" if you detect one.

15. A buyer for the exclusive Britique Shop purchased 100 cashmere pullover sweaters at ₹ 41 each and priced them at ₹ 90 retail. Also planned is a purchase of 72 shetland/ mohair blend bulk knit pullovers to retail at ₹ 50 each. Departmental goal markup is 51.8%. How much can be paid for each shetland/mohair pullover?

16. Determine the initial markup for a designer boutique that has the following projections for the next season:

    Planned sales = 40,00,000

    Markdowns = 6,00,000

    Expenses = 38%

    Cash discounts = 4%

    Shortages = 20,000

    Profit = 5%

17. What is the cumulative markup to date for an accessories department whose figures are:

Cost	Retail	
Opening Inventory	3,60,000	7,80,000
Purchases X	60,700	1,20,500
Purchases Y	1,20,000	2,45,000
Purchases Z	1,50,000	3,25,000

18. A shoe department with an initial markup of 53.2% had total retail reductions of 12%. What maintained markup was achieved in this department?

19. A luggage buyer plans a European buying trip to purchase ₹ 2,50,000 (cost value) of assorted travel packs. On the first stop in London, orders are placed for 1,92,000 (at cost) for an assortment of leather luggage, which will be priced at §180.000 retail. If the average markup is targeted at 52%, what markup percentage should now be taken on the balance of the European orders?

20. A buyer needs 5,000 umbrellas for the 37th annual stonewide 'April Showers" promotional event, to retail at ₹ 14 each. The planned markup is 49%. If 3,500 units are bought at one resource for ₹ 7.70 each, how much can the buyer afford to pay for each of the remaining 1,500 units?

3.5 ACTIVITY

1. Discuss markup, markdown and employees discount and play roles of a retailer, manager, customer to increase profits.
2. Go to nearest reliance store and discuss the issues of customer returns and allowances with a manager.
3. Do you think customer returns, employees discount and markdown are necessary evils, write a report and discuss in the class.
4. Use your PC and open excel. Draw a six months plan for your retail shop. Let there be three products, decide your own figures for markdown and markups
5. Find out the difference in profits when two products are sold as bundles. You can assume the prices and cost of two products and volumes? Does bundling help to increase profits?

4 CHAPTER

Retail Method of Inventory

4.1 LEARNING OBJECTIVES

You will learn

1. How to manage inventory?
2. How to plan inventory?
3. How to value inventory?

Retail Inventory Management

Retail inventory management is probably one of the most complex of all inventory management departments. In retail management, retailer will have a greater variety of products to store and a great deal more of each product. In fact, retiler's warehouse may never be big enough to hold all the merchandise that he needs to keep in stock, and it can be difficult to maintain the right number of any particular item at any given time.

Retail inventory management should never be the job of a single individual but should be divided into departments and classified accordingly. For example, in a supermarket, you'll have two major departments – grocery and nongrocery – and each will have several subcategories. Under grocery, you can expect such departments as meat, dairy, frozen, canned and more.

Delegation of Responsibility

Depending on the size of your store, your retail inventory management could be divided into the two main categories and delegated to two individuals who would be responsible for the management of your entire inventory, or you could break it down further, having an employee in charge of each smaller division. This would allow the individual to gain an intimate knowledge of how quickly each product sold and how often it needed to be reordered. This would easily allow you to account for excess stock in some areas while others remained fairly empty. Being efficient in carefully stocking the storage areas, as well as knowing what your best sellers are, can help you keep your retail inventory management process strong and in balance.

You are in trouble if you have to keep telling customers, "I'm sorry we're out of that size. May we order it for you?" Even though the shirts are selling briskly, you will lose customers if you don't have an item in stock. When the customer spends, you have got to be ready with the goods. This is what inventory management is all about. In many retail and wholesale operations, the single largest asset is inventory. Control of this investment is vital. It will eliminate a number of the problems associated with capital shortages and will also provide capital to permit expansion of operations for increased sales and profit.

Need for Prompt Action

Inventory problems often require prompt corrective action. In many businesses, the market life of inventory is short and if inventory is insufficient when market demand peaks, sales and profits are lost. If inventory is excessive when demand declines, the excess must be cleared, often at sharply reduced prices, again affecting profits.

These special problems are particularly acute in certain businesses. The market life for the latest hit record may be just a few months. For seasonal greeting cards, the market life is a few weeks, and for fresh fruit, produce and baked goods, the market life is measured in days.

Controlling Inventory Levels

You can control the inventory levels in your business to provide a suitable assortment and supply to meet market requirements while minimizing the risk of excessive investments. This can be accomplished by:

- Investing in inventory wisely so that excessive capital is not tied up, excessive space is not required, and the investment does not force unnecessary borrowing and interest expense.
- Maintaining accurate, up to date records to help identify and prevent shortages and to serve as a database for decisions.
- Taking prompt action to correct inventory imbalances.

Inventory Management

Inventory management can be briefly described as

- acquiring an adequate supply and assortment of merchandise from which customers can buy.
- Providing safety stocks to meet unexpected demand or delays in inventory replenishment.

- Maintaining clear, correct, and current records.
- Purchasing the proper assortment of goods in quantities that will maintain inventory levels consistent with business requirements, while providing adequate safety stocks.
- Reducing excessive inventories promptly, so that the rupees realized from clearing overstocks can be invested in merchandise with a greater market potential.

Inventory Investment Control

Inventory investment control is accomplished in two ways:

- Prompt elimination of overstocked items.
- Inventory replenishment in anticipation of customer demand.

Whenever a particular item is overstocked, the overstock should be reduced as promptly as possible. Naturally, the most effective and profitable way is to sell it to customers, even at a discount. However, there are other possibilities. There may be a wholesale market available for certain kinds of inventory. Excessive consumer goods inventories are often sold to "bargain basements" or warehouse outlets. Perhaps you can even arrange wholesale sales to a competitor. Frequently, it is wiser to scrap inventory that shows no sales activity for an extended period of time. In this way, you reduce a misleading overstatement of inventory on your company's books. At the same time, you make space available for inventory that can be sold at a profit.

Inventory Replenishment

The key to successful inventory management is adherence to procedures for inventory replenishment. Your ability to anticipate customer demand for certain items will help you plan your inventory purchases so that sufficient stocks are on hand to accommodate sales volume without excesses that cause other problems. Planning your purchases will also help you avoid shortages that can only be filled through forfeiture of discounts or absorption of premium shipping charges.

Determining purchasing requirements involves answering two questions:

- What to buy?
- How much to buy?

Both questions can be answered by establishing an inventory target for any item you carry expressed as so many days', weeks', or months' sales. For example, if a grocery store planned to carry a two days' supply of muffins, and average daily sales were 15 boxes of muffins, then a desirable inventory level could be calculated as follows:

Inventory Level = Days' Supply × Average Daily Sales

Inventory Level = 2 × 15

Inventory Level = 30

If the supply on hand is less than 30 boxes, then more muffins must be purchased. If the actual stock were 17 boxes, then the grocer would have to purchase 13 = (30 – 17) boxes.

The example of the grocer is relatively simple. Purchases are made directly from the truck. Sales in the last few days are a reasonable indicator of sales in the next two days. There is no waiting period for deliveries and supply is reliable. In many businesses, the problem becomes far more complex. In any business, an appropriate inventory level should be calculated by considering expected sales in the coming period. For products that show a steady sales pattern regardless of season or current fads, this can be based upon average monthly sales.

Sales Forecasting

The first step in estimating expected sales in coming months is to calculate, from inventory records, actual sales during an appropriate review period. For example, if you want to determine an appropriate inventory level for ski boots on October 1, it will be of little value to consider sales in July, August, or September. Average monthly sales for the entire year will tell you little or nothing either. A more suitable review period would be the months of October, November, and December of the previous year. In addition, if your sales showed a year to year growth rate, you should adjust review period sales for the average sales growth that your business has experienced in the previous year. Consider the following example. A sporting goods store desires to maintain a three months' supply of ski boots in inventory. On October 1, the store is determining a suitable inventory level so that an order can be prepared to build inventory to the three month level. Sales of ski boots have increased 20% from year to year. Sales in October, November and December of the previous year were as follows:

October > 5

November > 10

December > 20

Adding 20% to each of these amounts to reflect sales growth, expected sales for the present year would be as follows:

October > 6

November > 12

December > 24

Expected sales for the three month period would then be 42 (6 + 12 + 24). Therefore, the store should try to have this quantity in inventory on October 1. Another factor that should be considered in demand forecasting is whether or not stock outs that prevented a customer request from being fulfilled affected sales during the review period. Forecasting requires measurement of customer demand for a particular item, the number of pieces that customers wished to purchase, not just those orders that you were able to sell. If information is available, such requests should be added to actual sales for the review period in order to reach a more realistic estimate of demand for the coming months.

In some businesses, accurate records are maintained of all unfulfilled customer requests. This permits management to establish more accurate demand figures in determining inventory replenishment requirements and making decisions to add new items to inventory.

4.2 ESTABLISHING INVENTORY GUIDELINES

In some cases, product shelf life may be the determining factor. If the grocer stocked more than a two days' supply of muffins, they would lose their freshness and the grocer would lose customers. Delivery is immediate. The grocer gives the order directly to the bakery truck driver and the driver fills the order in minutes. More often, there are many other factors to consider. Take the case of the retailer who may require two weeks to receive delivery from suppliers on most items. On an emergency basis, the retailer may be able to replenish inventory more promptly, but only by forfeiting quantity discounts or incurring extra delivery charges. For most items, it is better to accept normal delivery, taking full advantage of all available discounts and minimizing freight charges. The length of time between order placement and receipt of goods is called lead time. If the lead time were two weeks, would it be sufficient to establish a minimum inventory level of a two weeks' supply? Probably not. If no order was placed until the supply of a certain item reached two weeks, there would probably be just enough stock on hand to cover expected sales until the order arrived. However, if anything went wrong (and it usually does), there would be a stock out before the order was received. An unexpectedly large request from a customer might not be filled because of insufficient inventory. A strike, shipping delays, manufacturing problems, or unforeseen weather conditions could seriously delay the arrival of the merchandise so that the stock out could last for several weeks. Therefore, most businesses maintain a safety, or cushion stock as protection against such occurrences. The size of the safety stock will depend upon the number and extent of the factors that could interrupt deliveries. Suitable guidelines would have to be based upon your own experience in the industry. Additionally, many items require a basic stock, an amount sufficient to accommodate regular sales, offering customers a reasonable assortment of merchandise from which their selection can be made. Assume that the lead time for a particular item is two weeks. The safety stock that the business wishes to maintain is a four weeks' supply. Additionally, a one week basic stock is required. The desired inventory level would be established as the sum of these factors:

Lead Time is 2 weeks + Safety Stock 4 weeks + Basic Stock 1 week = Inventory Level 7 weeks

What to Buy?

The desired inventory level should be considered an order point. Whenever the stock of an item falls below this point, it should be ordered. For example, if a camera shop wishes to maintain a 10 weeks' supply of film in inventory and average sales of a particular film type are 50 rolls per week, the order point would be 500 (50 × 10) rolls. When inventory drops below 500 rolls, more film should be ordered.

How Much to Buy?

The quantity of film to purchase would depend upon the usual time between orders, called the ordering interval. In this way, sufficient supplies would be maintained so that inventories between orders would average out to the desired level. A stock equal to expected sales during the camera shop's two week order interval should be added to the order point in order to determine the order ceiling.

Order Ceiling = Order Point + Order Interval Sales

Order Ceiling = 500 + (50 × 2)

Order Ceiling = 600

An order quantity could then be determined as follows, assuming 450 rolls are on hand:

Order Quantity = Order Ceiling – Stock on Hand

Order Quantity = 600 – 450

Order Quantity = 150 rolls

If an order for 50 rolls had already been placed, but not yet received, the present order should be reduced by the 50 rolls on order. The new order would then be 100 (150 – 50) rolls.

Let us review the steps involved in establishing order quantities using a hardware store as an example. The store desires to maintain a basic tool stock equal to one week's sales and a safety stock of one week's sales. Lead-time for order placement and delivery is two weeks. Orders are placed every four weeks. A desirable inventory level, or order point, is then calculated as follows:

Lead Time 2 weeks

+ Basic Stock 1 week

+ Safety Stock 1 week

= Order Point 4 weeks or 12 (4 × 3) saws

Whenever the supply of any tool drops to a four weeks' supply or below, an order should be placed.

To determine the order quantity, you must first calculate the order ceiling:

Order Point 4 weeks

+ Order Interval 4 weeks

= Order Ceiling 8 weeks or 24 (8 × 3) saws

Assume that an order is being prepared for saws. Average weekly sales are 3 saws and the stock on hand is 10 saws. This is below the order point of 12 (4 × 3) saws. The order quantity would then be calculated as follows:

Order Ceiling 24 – Stock on Hand 10 = Order Quantity 14

The hardware store should order 14 saws. If any are already on order, the outstanding order quantity should be subtracted.

Other Ordering Considerations

No business can be run by formulas alone. But formulas can be useful in guiding decisions. Before straying from them, you should be sure to have good and sufficient reason. One common reason for straying from the ordering formulas previously described is the availability of quantity discounts and price specials. Naturally, you want to take advantage of these potential savings whenever possible. However, if quantity discounts force you to order far more than you need, the discount you earn may later be lost when you are forced to close out the merchandise at distress prices.

Maintaining Control

Systematic review of inventory purchases is the most effective means of preventing overstocks and avoiding lost sales. The availability of accurate inventory and sales records, combined with your own judgment, can guide you to sound purchasing decisions.

Periodic Inventory Changes

Inventory levels are constantly changing. As goods are purchased or produced, inventories increase. As goods are sold, inventories are reduced. To determine the inventory at the end of any period, you begin with the inventory on hand at the beginning of the period. Then, the ending inventory can be calculated as follows:

Opening Inventory + Additions to Inventory during the period – Deductions from Inventory during the period = Ending Inventory

For example, a wholesaler of furniture has 100 mattresses in inventory on April 1. During the month, 50 mattresses are received and 2 are returned from customers. Total additions to inventory for the month would be:

50 Productions + 2 Returns = 52 Total Additions

Sales of mattresses during the month are 40 and 1 must be scrapped because of warehouse handling damage. Total deductions from inventory would then be as follows:

40 Sales + 1 Scrapped = 41 Total Deductions

The closing inventory on April 30 can then be calculated as follows:

100 Opening Inventory, April 1

+ 52 Additions to Inventory, April

– 41 Deductions from Inventory, April

= 111 Closing Inventory, April 30

Additions to inventory normally include the following:

- Purchases
- Returns from customers

Deductions from inventory normally include:

- Sales
- Returns to vendors
- Scrappage
- Pilferage
- Inventory adjustments

4.3 INVENTORY VALUATION

Inventory calculations, based upon units, are useful when determining the inventory of a particular item. More often, however, you will want to know the rupee value of inventory, particularly your total inventory. Total inventory can be evaluated in total rupee s only since it usually includes a mix of various items such as apples and oranges, which cannot be added together.

Valuation at Cost

In most businesses, inventories are valued at cost. For example, an appliance retailer purchases hair dryers for ₹ 7.50 each and sells them for ₹ 13.50 each. The value assigned to each hair drier in inventory would be ₹ 7.50. The exception to this rule occurs in some retailing activities, where many retailers find it more convenient to evaluate the inventory at the retail price since this permits easier calculation of such figures as markups, markdowns, and expenses as a percentage of sales. When calculating the value of inventory, consistency requires that all factors be evaluated on the same basis. If inventory is valued at cost, purchases must be entered at cost when determining deductions. If inventory is valued at retail, sales and receipts must also be measured at retail.

A school supplies distributor has a beginning inventory on June 1 of ₹ 2,00,000. During the month, sales are ₹ 50,000. The cost of these sales is ₹ 35,000. New supplies are received with a cost of ₹ 40,000. You would calculate the June 30 inventory as follows:

Beginning Inventory ₹ 2,00,000 + Production 40,000 – Sales 35,000

= Ending Inventory ₹ 2,05,000

Note that sales are recorded at cost, not actual selling prices, to be consistent with the wholesaler's inventory valuation basis.

Successful merchandising requires that the size of stocks offered the consumer be large enough to satisfy demand, but that the investment be kept as low as possible. This can be accomplished only by having a frequent indication of stock on hand. The retail merchandiser who is concerned with the question "How much can I sell?" must know how much to buy to maintain this satisfactory relationship between the amount of sales volume and the size of stocks carried. In recent years, the increased use of computer information systems by department stores, small retail businesses, and most merchandising chains has had a major impact on the management of merchandise inventories and other areas of record keeping.

The retail method of inventory is a method of averages, with the retail stock figure at the end of an accounting period providing the basis for determining the cost value of stock. The conversion of the closing inventory at retail to a cost figure is calculated by the determination of the cumulative markup percentage on the total merchandise handled. To understand the retail method of inventory, it is vital to realize that it operates on the theory that the merchandise in stock is always representative of the total merchandise handled to date (i.e., stock plus new purchases). It allows an acceptable cost value of the book inventory to be established so that gross margin can be determined periodically.

4.4 THE RETAIL METHOD OF INVENTORY

The retail system of merchandise accounting permits the retailer to determine the value (at retail) of the stock on hand at frequent and periodic intervals without taking constant physical counts. However, it must be noted that periodic — generally semi annual — physical counts (i.e., inventories) are taken at the current retail prices of the merchandise on hand. To control stocks and determine the profitability of individual departments, the retail method of accounting is applied separately for each department. The retail method of inventory valuation involves:

- Taking a physical inventory count to determine the total retail value of a particular department.
- Determining the cumulative markup percentage on the total merchandise handled.
- Deriving the cost value of the closing inventory from the retail by using the cumulative markup percentage achieved on the total merchandise handled. Subsequently, this valuation is used to find the cost of goods sold to establish the gross margin.

The computation from "statistical records" or book figures of the amount of merchandise that should be on hand, at retail, is called a book inventory. At the beginning of the accounting period under consideration, a physical inventory count is taken at the current retail price of the goods owned. It is common that when large stores take a semi annual physical count of stocks and record the value at retail, that date of receipt of merchandise into stock is also recorded.

When taking a physical inventory using this method, it is not necessary to list the cost price of each individual item. The physical count of each individual item, at the retail price stated on its ticket, is recorded and the total retail figure is the actual amount of goods accounted for at the time the semi annual count is made. If warranted, this count can be made more often. This actual physical count figure is then used as the closing physical stock figure for that accounting period. If the physical inventory value is less than the book inventory, the difference is called a shortage. **When the physical inventory value exceeds the book inventory, that difference is called an overage.**

Maintaining a Perpetual Book Inventory Figure

A book inventory indicates the amount of stock in rupees that has been determined from records rather than from an actual count. During the time period between the semi annual physical counts just described, many other merchandising transactions occur, such as:

- Goods are sold to customers.
- Merchandise is purchased and received from resources.
- Customers return merchandise.
- Merchandise is marked down.
- Goods are transferred to other departments in the same store for resale.
- Merchandise is transferred to other stores.
- Merchandise is returned to vendors occasionally

Every such transaction and any other kind of merchandise movement is accompanied by paperwork in the form of sales checks, return to vendor forms, orders, and so on. The retail organization's statistical department or the accounting division records every transaction and adds to or reduces the "book accordingly. For example, sales to customers or transfers to other department reduce the "book stock" (also known as perpetual or running book inventory) by the amount corresponding to the retail value of the goods: or transferred. The records must be current and accurate so that a retail inventory figure is always available during an accounting period. Any addition to or deductions from stock must be recorded as the current retail prices; reported to the statistical department. In other words, every change that affects the stock value must be recorded.

The accurate determination of stock on hand periodically maintains the proper relationship between sales and stock as merchandise purchases are controlled in ratio to ample stocks. The estimation of profits at any given time allows the timely correction of any adverse conditions. The maximization of possible insurance claims by providing acceptable, accurate records of inventory validation.

The following is an example of a department for a branch store, which should serve to illustrate the "addition or deduction" of the value of the merchandise in stock. All these changes must be recorded to ensure accuracy.

Increase in Retail Value		Decrease in Retail Value	
Purchases	35,000	Net sales	28,000
Transfers in Retails	5,000	Transfer out Retails	2,000
	Returns to vendors	3,000	
	Employees discount	500	
	MD differences	500	
Total Stock additions (Total ins)	40,000	Total Stock deductions (Total outs)	34,000

Book Inventory Figure at Retail

A retail book inventory is determined by:

- Taking a periodic physical count, at retail, to determine a closing physical stock figure.
- Establishing the physical count amount as the opening retail book inventory.
- Adding all new purchases at retail to determine the total merchandise handled at retail.
- Subtracting all retail deductions (e.g., net sales, markdowns, etc.) from the retail total merchandise handled to find the closing book inventory at retail.

4.4.1 Solved Example

On January 31, the physical count of the infants' department in Branch #15 revealed an inventory of ₹ 20,000. On February 1, the opening retail inventory of this department was ₹ 20,000. From February 1 to July 31 retail purchases amounting to ₹ 40,000 were received. The net sales for this period were ₹ 30,500, the markdowns taken were ₹ 2,300, employee discounts were ₹ 200, returns to vendors were ₹ 350, and transfers out were ₹ 750. What was the retail book inventory for this period under consideration?

Solution:

Opening book retail inventory (Feb. 1)	20,000
+ Retail purchases (Feb. 1-July31)	+ 40,000
Total merchandise handled (ins)	60,000
Net sales =	30,500
+ Markdown differences =	2,300

+ Employee discounts =	200
+ Returns to vendor =	350
+ Transfers out =	750
Total deductions (outs) =	–34,100
Retail Book Inventory =	25,900

A book inventory, at cost, is determined by:

- Converting the opening retail book inventory to a cost inventory figure by using the cumulative markup percentage achieved on the stock plus purchases during the previous accounting period.
- Adding all new purchases, at cost, plus freight (on cost only) to the cost opening inventory figure to determine the total merchandise handled at cost.

4.4.2 Solved Example

Calculate a book inventory at cost, if the markup percentage on the previous season's inventory is 51% and the cost of the new purchases is 19,800. Use other figures as in earlier solved problem

Solution:

1. Convert opening book retail inventory figure to cost inventory figure.

   Opening cost inventory = 20,000 R × (100% – MU%)

   = 20,000 × (100% – 51%)

   = 20,000 × 49%

   = 9,800

2. Add all new purchases plus freight to opening inventory at cost. Given-.

   New purchases, at cost = 19,800

   + Freight = + 200

   Total = 20,000

   Opening inventory at cost = 9,800

   New purchases (including freight) at cost = + 20,000

   Total merchandise handled at cost = 29,800

3. Find cumulative markup percentage on total merchandise handled.

	Cost	Retail
Opening inventory	9,800	20,000
Purchases	20,000	40,000
Total Merchandise	29,800	60,000

Markup = 60,000 – 29,800 = 30,200

Markup %age = 30,200/60,000 = 50.3%

4. Convert closing book inventory at retail to closing book inventory at cost by using the cumulative MU percentage.

Closing book inventory at retail = 25,900

25,900 × (100% – 50.35%) = 25,900 × 49.7%

Closing Book Inventory at Cost = 12,872.30

Forms Used in the Retail Method of Inventory

Today a retailer's records are often supplemented and/or obtained through the store's (or organization's) computer system (e.g., POS markdowns). How the information is recorded is a matter of choice or monetary necessity, but the loss of records or the failure to record the proper information that shows the increase or decrease in the value of the stock will result in an inaccurate stock valuation of the book inventory. There are many forms to help the retailer accurately record this valuable information. Each form serves a particular function, but not all retailers use identical forms. The forms in this section illustrate the function of each record required to appreciate or depreciate the value of a stock. Today, with the widespread use of automated merchandising systems, the information necessary to maintain an accurate recording of transactions is adopted and tailored to each retailer's needs.

Purchase Record

Purchase Record provides a record of the billed or invoiced costs, transportation charges, cash discounts, retail amounts, and the percentages of markup for each individual purchase. The names of the vendors, dates of invoices, and the invoice numbers are also entered. Each department checks this record periodically to ensure that the department is being charged or credited with merchandise either entering or leaving a department and that these amounts are only intended for that department. The report also shows the department classification, vendor, style and price receipts in units for the total store as well as individual branches. The negative units represent returns to vendors or corrections. The purpose of the report is to allow buyers to examine receipts entered into the computer against copies of the purchase order. Discrepancies are then reported so that appropriate adjustments can be made.

Transfer of Goods

A transfer of merchandise involves the movement of goods. When the merchandise leaves a department, the transfer is out; conversely, when the merchandise is received, the transfer is in. When merchandise is transferred from one store to another (e.g., a branch), an Outstanding Transfer List Form is used to record the number of units transferred, unit cost, total cost, unit retail, and total retail. Merchandise may also be transferred from one department to an other. This record is used to indicate the change of ownership of merchandise.

Price Change Forms

All retail price changes that are required to merchandise a department must be recorded. Among the changes necessary to record are:

- The number of units.
- The old retail price per unit.
- The new retail price per unit.
- The difference per unit.
- The total amount of difference.

Today it is common that temporary price changes (e.g., one day sale items) are recorded by a cash register at the time of the purchase. This is called a point of sale markdown (POS). When a consumer pays for a purchase, the pre-programmed cash register records the new or lower retail, which corresponds exactly with the prescribed reduction posted on signs displayed with the merchandise. Only permanent reductions are recorded manually on forms

Charge Back to Vendors

A debit memo form records the return of merchandise from the retailer to the vendor, which may occur for a variety of reasons. It displays the number of pieces or units, the name of the item, and both cost and retail prices. Typically, a worksheet, is used to record the return to vendor information before it is verified by the person packing the merchandise. This ensures that the actual debit memo is legible and correct.

4.5 SHORTAGES AND OVERAGES

Physical inventories at current retail prices are taken at the end of the accounting period. At this same time, the "book stock" at retail is adjusted to agree with the value of the physical count. Any discrepancy between the amount of the "book stock" and the value of stock determined by the physical count of merchandise on hand is classified as a shortage (or shrinkage) or an overage. As described, **shortages exist if physical inventory is lower than book inventory; overages exist if the physical count exceeds the statistical tally.**

It is almost impossible to run a merchandising operation with 100% accuracy. Shortages or overages nearly always result and are actually expected to occur. The shortage or overage is commonly expressed as a percentage of the net sales. Regardless of the cause, the inventory shortage is fundamentally the buyer's or department manager's problem and responsibility. To keep discrepancies to a minimum is one of the many challenges a merchant must face. For internal control purposes, it is sometimes desirable to estimate shortages. This estimate is also expressed as a percentage of net sales. Furthermore, even though merchandise planning is devised with estimated planned shortages in mind, generally the actual shortage exceeds the expected shortage.

4.5.1 Causes of Shortages and Overages

Shortages may stem from inaccurate record keeping and/or faulty physical counts. A principal cause of shortages is pilferage which, realistically, can never be prevented completely Overages, however, can only be caused by faulty record keeping.

The common causes of shortages and overages are:

- Clerical errors in the calculation of the book and/or physical inventory which include: Failure to record markdowns properly. Incorrect "retailing" of invoices. Errors in charging invoices to departments. Errors in recording transfers. Errors in recording returns to vendor. Errors in recording physical inventory.
- Physical merchandise losses, which include: Theft by customers and/or employees. Unrecorded breakage and spoilage. Sales clerks' errors in recording sales. Overweighting. Borrowed merchandise. Lost or incorrect price tickets. Sampling.

Calculating Shortages and Overages

Shortage (or Overage) = Closing book inventory at retail – Physical inventory

4.5.1.1 Solved Example

Find the shortage or overage in rupees from the following figures;

Opening inventory at retail ₹ 22,000

Purchases at retail 17,500

Net sales 18,000

Markdowns 300

Employee discounts 600

Physical inventory, end of period 19,200

Solution:

Opening book inventory retail (ins) = ₹ 22,000

+ Purchases retail = +17,500

Total merchandise handled (total ins) = ₹ 39,500

Net sales + Markdown + Employee discounts (Total deductions (outs))

= ₹ 18,000 + 300 + 600 = ₹ 18,900

Book inventory retail = 39,500 – 18,900 = ₹ 20,600

– Physical inventory = –19,200

Rupees shortage = ₹ 1,400

4.5.3 The Advantages of the Retail Method of Inventory

The benefits of the retail method of inventory are that:

- It permits control over profit because the figures for markup obtained (i.e., the difference between the cost and the retail of the total merchandise handled) and markdowns taken (upon which the realized gross margin depends) frequently are available and immediate action can be taken to protect the desired profit margin.
- It simplifies the physical inventory process because the physical inventory is taken at retail prices, which is less difficult and less expensive. Additionally, because all entries are made rapidly and no decoding is necessary, the personnel used does not require special training or experience.
- It provides a book inventory and, therefore, discrepancies (i.e., shortages and/or overages) in stock can be determined, shortage causes may be discovered, and preventive/corrective measures can be taken.
- It provides an equitable basis for insurance and adjustment claims.

4.5.4 The Limitations of the Retail Method of Inventory

The disadvantages of the retail method of inventory are that:

- It is a system of averages and therefore does not provide a precise cost evaluation of the inventory at its present cost price. This figure (i.e., cost evaluation of inventory) is calculated by applying the markup complement percentage to the retail value of the inventory. This may result in a figure that is either greater or smaller than the invoice cost of the merchandise currently received. This is the most significant weakness of this method.

- It depends upon extensive record keeping for system accuracy.
- It is essential that all price changes be recorded.

Finding the Cost of Goods Sold and the Gross Margin with the Retail Method of Inventory Valuation

The retail method of inventory was introduced in department stores because it allowed a more simplified method to constantly monitor the all important gross margin figure. The retail method of inventory eliminated a whole system of records formerly necessary to determine the valuation of an inventory at cost.

4.5.4.1 Solved Example

A junior sportswear buyer wants to calculate the gross margin figure to ascertain whether the department is "on target" and will achieve the planned gross margin goals for the season. The available season to date information is:

Cost	Retail	MU%
Opening inventory	₹ 1,00,000	51%
New purchases and freight	2, 40,000	5,00,000

(Net Sales 4,25,000, Markdown ₹ 45,000 and shortages ₹ 5,000, cash discounts ₹ 13,000)

Step 1: Begin with a retail opening inventory figure: ₹ 1,00,000. The opening inventory at retail (₹ 1,00,000) was determined when the stock on hand was physically counted at the end of the previous accounting period. The cumulative markup of 51% was achieved.

Step 2: Determine a cost opening book inventory figure:

₹ 1,00,000 × (100% – 51%) = ₹ 1,00,000 × 49% = ₹ 49,000

Step 3: All new purchases (₹ 2,40,000 cost, ₹ 5,00,000 retail) are added to the opening book inventory figures (₹ 49,000 cost, ₹ 1,00,000 retail) to find total merchandise handled (TMH) figures (₹ 2,89,000 at cost and ₹ 6,00,000 at retail) resulting in a 51.8% cumulative markup.

Step 4: The sum ₹ 4,75,000 (₹ 4,25,000 total of net sales) + ₹ 45,000 (markdowns) + ₹ 5,000 (shortages) is subtracted from the retail figure of TMH (₹ 6,00,000) to find the retail closing book inventory figure (₹ 1,25,000).

Step 5: Determine a cost closing book inventory figure:

₹ 1,25,000 × (100% – 51.8%) = ₹ 1,25,000 × 48.2% = ₹ 60,250

Step 6: The closing book inventory at cost (₹ 60,250) is subtracted from TMH at cost (₹ 2,89,000) to find the cost of goods sold (₹ 2,28,750).

Step 7: The cost of goods sold (₹ 2,28,750) is then subtracted from the net sales (₹ 4,25,000) to find the merchandise margin (₹ 1,96,250).

Step 8: The cash discounts (₹ 13,000) are added to the merchandise margin (₹ 1,96,250), which equals ₹ 2,09,250.

Step 9: The workroom costs (₹ 1,000) are subtracted from ₹ 2,09,250 to find the gross margin (₹ 2,08,250).

From an accounting viewpoint, in the calculation of gross margin, the cash dis-counts and workroom costs are adjusted after the margin on the merchandise itself (i.e., maintained markup) is determined. Nonetheless, because merchants frequently negotiate cash discounts or influence the workroom factor, their impact on the gross margin must be considered.

4.6 PROBLEMS FOR PRACTICE

1. On Jan. 15, a statistical inventory indicates an on hand retail stock of ₹ 64,250. physical count on that date reveals a stock of ₹ 62,875. What is the opening retail book inventory figure for the period commencing Jan 16?
2. Opening inventory at retail for an outerwear department is ₹ 1,75,000. Purchases retail for the following six month period are 490,000, net sales are 4,00,000, markdowns are 30,000, returns to vendors are ₹ 10,000, transfers (transfers out) to the third floor boutique are ₹ 15,000, and employee discounts are ₹ 6,000. Find retail book inventory at the end of this six-month period.
3. Using the following figures from an accessories department, find the closing book stock at retail.

Physical inventory January 15	₹ 85,000
Purchases retail January 16 through July 15,	₹ 1,65,000
Gross sales	1,70,000
Returns from customers	30,000
Returns to vendors	5,000
Markdowns	10,000

4. The following figures are from a small boutique, which has a 49% MU:

Opening book inventory at retail	₹ 16,000
Net sales	31,000
Markdowns	2,000
Purchases (retail)	40,000

(a) Determine the retail book inventory for the period.

(b) Convert the closing retail book inventory figure to the cost value.

5. A lingerie department buyer was given the following data:

	Cost	Retail
Opening inventory	3,20,000	5,30,000
Purchases	11,18,000	22,71,000
Net sales		14,00,000
Markdowns (incl. empl. disc.)		90,000

Calculate

(a) The closing book inventory at retail.

(b) The closing book inventory at cost.

6. The athletic footwear department had a closing book inventory, at retail, of ₹ 4,00,000 and had achieved a 53.5% markup on total merchandise handled. Determine the closing inventory at cost.

7. Find the closing inventory, at cost, of a furniture department, if:

	Cost	Retail
Net sales		₹ 3,30,000
Opening inventory	₹ 1,50,000	3,25,000
Markdowns		25,000
Return to vendors	13,000	18,000
Employee discounts		6,500
Gross purchases	2,00,000	3,90,000

8. A costume jewellery department showed the following figures for a six month period:

Net sales	₹ 1,25,000
Purchases (at retail)	1,05,000
Opening retail inventory (Feb. 1)	64,000
Markdowns	9,000
Employee discounts	2,600
Physical count (July 31)	31,000

(a) What was the shortage in rupees?

(b) What was the shortage in percentage?

If the planned shortage was estimated at 2%, was the actual shortage more or less? By how much in rupees? In percentage?

9. Find the shortage or overage percentage if:

Net sales	₹ 1,37,000
Opening inventory (retail)	1,40,000
Markdowns	7,000
Employee discounts	1,000
Retail purchases	96,000
Closing physical inventory	89,150

10. Last year, the net sales in a home fashions department were ₹ 3,65,000. The book inventory at year end was ₹ 67,500, and the physical inventory was ₹ 66,000. What was the shortage percentage?

11. A new shop owner was reviewing figures with the store's accountant. Net sales for the first three months of business were ₹ 87,000 and the book inventory was ₹ 72,000. It was noted that the physical inventory was 2.5% lower than the book inventory. Find the shortage percentage for this three month period.

12. The coat department's net sales were ₹ 2,25,000, markdowns taken amounted to ₹ 15,000, and employee discounts were ₹ 3,000. The retail opening inventory for this period was ₹ 75,000, the purchases made at retail were ₹ 2,10,000, and the buyer estimated the shortages at 296. Determine the estimated physical count.

13. A store with net sales of ₹ 35,00,000 has estimated its shortages to be 2%. The actual rupee shortage amounted to ₹ 72,000.

    (a) Was this shortage a higher or lower percentage than anticipated? By how much?

    (b) What was the rupee difference between the estimated and the actual shortage?

14. The net sales of a lingerie department were ₹ 2,95,000; inventory on February 1 was ₹ 1,50,000; markdowns were 8% of net sales; purchases for this period were ₹ 3,62,000; the physical inventory taken July 31 was ₹ 1,88,400.

    (a) Was there a rupee shortage for this period?

    (b) What was the shortage or overage percentage for this period?

15. A men's outerwear department had an opening inventory of ₹ 3,40,000. The net purchases were ₹ 78,000, gross sales were ₹ 1,40,250, customer returns were ₹ 11,150, and markdowns—including employee discounts—were ₹ 4,800. Shortages of 1.2% were estimated. Calculate:

    (a) The closing retail book inventory.

    (b) The estimated physical inventory

4.7 ACTIVITY

1. Interview a purchase manager of a retail organisation and discuss the benefits of inventory management
2. Take a good book. Read the concept of Economic Order Quantity. How can it be applicable to retail merchandise?
3. Work on excel spreadsheet and try various inventory levels to find out the effect on profitability.
4. Discuss the issues of shortages and overages in the class.
5. Just watch a medicine store keeper, how he writes the requirements when he sells one item to a customer.

CHAPTER 5

Rupee Planning and Control

5.1 LEARNING OBJECTIVES

As a device for unifying merchandising operations, the objectives of the rupee plan are:

- To procure a net profit by providing an instrument that plans, forecasts, and controls the purchase and sales of merchandise.
- To research previous results to repeat and improve prior successes and to avoid failures.
- To integrate the various merchandising activities involved in determining the purchases necessary to achieve the estimated planned sales

5.2 THE PROCEDURE OF RUPEE PLANNING BY ELEMENT

STEP 1

Carefully forecast future total sales volume in rupees for the entire period by:

(a) Reviewing and analyzing past sales performance for the same time period.

(b) Considering factors that may cause a change in sales. These factors include:

- Current sales trends.
- Previous rate of growth patterns.
- Economic conditions.
- Local business conditions.
- Fashion factors.

- Influencing conditions within and from outside the store or department, (e.g., changes in store concepts, market direction, competition, etc.).

(c) Establishing, for the season, a percentage of estimated sales change after analyzing the sales performance and current conditions that cause sales changes. Then, calculate the total sales volume for the period. The following calculations are used in this procedure.

A: Find out %age of sales increase.

5.2.1 Solved Example

If last year's actual sales were ₹ 18,34,900 and this year's planned sales are ₹ 20,00,000 what is the percentage of sales increase?

Solution:

Percentage sales increase = (20,00,000 – 18,34,900)/18,34,900*100

Sales increase percentage = 8.9% or 9%

B: To set the individual monthly sales goals, use the seasonal distribution of the previous year's sales for the same period as a guideline. When adjusting the planned monthly sales increase or decrease, the three essential processes that influence a buyer's judgment are:

- Considering the department's past experience with respect to the normal percentage distribution of sales for the planning period.
- Comparing the monthly percentage distribution with industry performance.
- Adjusting monthly sales figures because of shifting dates of certain holidays, planned special promotions, and other merchandising strategies.

C: Plan Stock

There is no formula to plan stock, it is subjective judgement and investment amount available.

In the planning and control of stocks, every merchandiser's objective is to:

- Maintain adequate assortments (i.e., reasonably complete from a customer's viewpoint).
- Regulate the investment of stocks in relation to sales to obtain a satisfactory balance between these two factors.

D: Determining the Turnover Figure

Every retailer should understand the importance of turnover to make better use of capital investment, to control inventories, and ultimately, to realize optimum profits. It acts as an index to efficient merchandising. Successful stock planning does not begin with turnover, but results in achieving the desired rate of stock turnover. This term indicates the number of times that an average stock is sold for a given period of time, which, unless otherwise stated, refers to a period of one year. However, turnover may be computed on a weekly, monthly, or seasonal basis. The actual number of stock turns varies with the type of merchandise and price.

Turnover is important to a merchandising operation because it:

- Stimulates sales by presenting fresh merchandise to the customer.
- Reduces markdowns by keeping the flow of new goods constant, thereby curbing the accumulation of large amounts of older stock.
- Lowers cost of goods sold because the "open-to-buy" position permits the buyer to take advantage of special prices and offerings.
- Decreases interest, merchandise taxes, and other operating expenses as a percentage of net sales.

Calculating Average Retail Stock when Monthly Inventories are known

The method of finding an average monthly inventory at cost is exactly the same as determining the average stock at retail.

Average retail stock = Sum of beginning inventories + Ending inventory for given period

5.2.2 Solved Example

Find the average retail stock and the turnover for this period.

Sales		BOM stocks	
January	₹ 10,000	Jan. 1	₹ 13,000
February	8,000	Feb. 1	12,000
March	14,000	Mar. 1	17,000
April	16,000	Apr. 1	19,000
May	12,000	May 1	15,000
June	14,000	June 1	18,000
July	10,000	July 1	14,000
August	6,000	Aug. 1	10,000
September	12,000	Sept. 1	16,000
October	11,000	Oct. 1	15,000
November	12,000	Nov. 1	15,000
December	15,000	Dec. 1	18,000
		Dec. 31(₹ 13,000 is ending inventory)	

Solution:

Sum of 12 BOM stocks			= ₹ 1,82,000
+ EOM stock			= + 13,000
			= 1,95,000
Average retail	stock		₹ 1,95,000 (Sum of 13 figures)

13 (Number of inventories)

Average retail stock for one year = 15,000

After calculating an average stock figure, the formula of net sales for the period under consideration divided by the average stock is applied to determine the turnover rate. For example:

Turnover = ₹ 1,40,000 (Sum of 12 monthly sales figures)/₹ 15,000 (Average retail stock for the period)

Turnover = 9.3

In planning stocks for a season, from the standpoint of stock turnover, merchandise is apportioned so that the average stock is related to the sales for the entire period. This approach does not offer a basis for planning a specific amount of stock to be on hand to achieve a planned sales figure.

5.3 DETERMINING GROSS MARGIN RETURN BY RUPEE INVENTORY

While retailers have stock turn goals to judge the efficiency of the balance between sales and stocks, when money is tight greater emphasis is placed on the relationship between the inventory investment, or working capital, and its ability to produce gross margins. The objective is to produce a maximum gross margin from a minimum amount of investment.

The ratio of productivity of each rupee invested in inventory is similar to a share of stock, and the productivity of this rupee is equivalent, to some degree, to earnings per share. Stock turnover influences and affects the utilization of money invested in inventory. The more times money is converted into sales and gross margin, the greater the return per rupee of inventory. Today, the frequency of this "reinvestment" is an increasingly significant factor. The measurement of the efficiency of investment in inventory is referred to as gross margin return per rupee of inventory, which is commonly known as GMROI. This element is used by financial analysts to measure capital turnover.

Merchandisers in retailing are responsible for a successful stock turnover and consequently are focused on it. Both stock turn and GMROI are involved with inventory productivity and the relationship between these two elements is that the calculation of stock turn utilizes an average inventory at retail, and GMROI uses an average inventory at cost.

5.3.1 Solved Example

The following example illustrates this concept:

Given:

Net sales = ₹ 12,00,000

Gross margin = 4,80,000

Average inventory (retail) = 4,80,000

Average inventory (cost) = 2,40,000

Find:

(a) Stock turnover = ₹ 12,00,000 Net sales/4,80,000 Average inventory at retail

= 2.5

(b) GMROI = 4,80,000 Gross margin/2,40,000 Average inventory at cost = 2.0

This is the simplest level of calculating GMROI. It is apparent that as more sales and gross margin rupees are generated, without increasing inventory, GMROI will increase.

It is more practical to think of GMROI in terms commonly used in merchandising. These factors, which can be managed and influenced, are:

- Markup percentage.
- Gross margin percentage.
- Turnover

5.3.2 Solved Example

The year to date results of the intimate apparent department are:

Gross margin: 40%

Turnover: 2.5

Markup: 50%

What is the GMROI achieved by this department?

Solution:

GMROI = (GM% * Turn Over)/(100-MU%)

= (40% G.M. × 2.5 TO)/(100% – 50% MU) = (.40 × 2.5)/(100% – 50%)

= 1/0.5 = 2

The GMROI result shows the relationship of the components and demonstrates how future results can be improved.

The key to successful retailing is achieving more rupee sales without a corresponding increase in inventory Through the determination of turnover, the stock level that produce an optional sales level can be measured. The calculation of GMROI shows the profitability or cash flow that these sales produce.

Calculating Stock Sales Ratio when Retail Stock and Sales for a given period are known

Stock sales ratio = Retail stock at given time in the period

Sales for the period

5.3.3 Solved Example

On a particular day, the boys' wear department had a retail stock of ₹ 1,20,000. The planned sales for the month were ₹ 20,000. Find the stock sales ratio for the month of February.

Solution:

Stock sales ratio = 1,20,000/20,000 = 6

The value placed on an inventory has a decided effect on profits. **The relationship between sales volume, cost of merchandise sold, given expenses, and the operating profit has been shown by following example, data has been used as shown in earlier examples.**

	Cost	Retail	% of sales
Net Sales		4,25,000	100
Opening book	49,000		
Inventory + Purchases	2,40,000		
Total Mer. Handled (TMH)	2,89,000		
– closing stock	– 60,250		
Gross cost of merc. sold	2,28,750		
– cash discount	13,000		
Net	2,15,750		
+ workroom	1,000		
Net cost of merc sold	2,16,750	– 2,16,750	– 51
Gross margin		2,08,250	49
– operating expenses		1,91,250	– 45
Net profit		17,000	4%

Setting Stock Figures by the Weeks Supply Method

The weeks supply method plans inventory size on a weekly basis. The set amount of stock equals a calculated number of weeks supply. The number of weeks supply that is to be "on hand" depends on the planned turnover figure to be achieved and is used as a guide to set the number of weeks inventory supply. This technique of stock planning is best used in a department that primarily carries staple merchandise and/or has a relatively stable sales volume. Note that because the stock size is in direct relation to the planned weekly sales, it can result in an excessive stock condition at the peak selling periods or in dangerously low stocks during the slower months.

Calculating the Number of Weeks Supply

Number of weeks supply = Weeks/Desired turnover

5.3.4 Solved Example

A Department has a planned stock turnover of 4.0 for the six month period. Determine the number of weeks supply needed to achieve the desired turnover.

Solution:

Number of weeks supply = 26 weeks (6 months)/4.0 turnover

Number of weeks supply = 6.5

Finding Planned Stock, Given Turnover, and Weekly Rate of Sales

Planned stock = Average weekly sales × Number of weeks supply

5.3.5 Solved Example

A department has an average weekly sales rate of ₹ 9,800 and a planned turnover of 4.0 for the six month period. Calculate the amount of stock to be carried.

Solution:

Step 1: Find the number of weeks supply given the turnover and the supply period.

Number of weeks supply = 26 weeks (6 months)/4.0 turnover

Number of weeks supply = 6.5

Step 2: Find planned stock given the average weekly sales and the number of weeks supply.

Planned stock = ₹ 9,800 Average weekly sales × 6.5 No. of weeks supply

Planned stock = ₹ 63,700

Setting Beginning of the Month Stock Figures by Basic Stock Method

Another approach to balancing stocks and sales is the basic stock method, which is the average inventory for the period. This average inventory is derived simply from the planned sales and turnover.

For example, if the anticipated six month sales total ₹ 9,60,000 and a turnover of 2 is desired for the season, average inventory can be calculated by applying the formula:

Sales/Average inventory Turnover = ₹ 9,60,000/2 = ₹ 4,80,000

This technique presumes that the retailer will begin each month with a minimum amount of basic stock that remains constant regardless of the monthly sales to be achieved. Generally, it is best to apply this basic stock (i.e., fixed quantity of stock maintained throughout the season) when the annual turnover rate is 6 or less because using it with higher stockturn merchandise would result in unrealistic basic stocks.

Finding a BOM Stock When a Basic Stock and Planned Sales for the Month are known

5.3.6 Solved Example

The calculated basic stock figure is added to each month's planned sales to determine the BOM amount for the month.

BOM stock = Basic stock + Planned sales for the month.

In an accessories department that has planned a turnover of 4 for the Fall season, the estimated sales are as follows:

August	₹ 28,000
September	30,000
October	32,000
November	36,000
December	40,000
January	26,000

Calculate the BOM stocks using the basic stock method.

Solution:

Step 1: Determine average monthly sales.

August ₹ 28,000

September 30,000

October 32,000

November 36,000

December 40,000

January 26,000

Total for the season = ₹ 1,92,000

Average monthly sales = 1,92,000/6 ₹ 32,000

Step 2: Calculate average inventory. **Average inventory** = ₹ 1,92,000 Sales/4 Turnover = ₹ 48,000

Step 3: Find basic stock.

Basic stock at retail = Average inventory ₹ 48,000

– Average monthly sales – 32,000

Basic stock = ₹ 16,000

Calculate BOM stock by adding basic stock to monthly planned sales

	Monthly sales	Basic Stock	BOM Stock
August	₹ 28,000 +	₹ 16,000	₹ 44,000
September	30,000 +	16,000	46,000
October	32,000 +	16,000	48,000
November	36,000 +	16,000	52,000
December	40,000 +	16,000	56,000
January	26,000 +	16,000	42,000

5.4 PLANNING MARKDOWNS

In rupee amount planning, markdowns are important because they reduce the total value of the stock available for sale. Careful planning of markdowns helps reduce the amount of markdowns taken, which helps increase net profit figures. The amount of planned markdowns to be taken is expressed both in rupees and as a percentage of planned sales. Because the rupee markdowns vary greatly, the percentage data is more significant for comparison between past and present performance. The percentage of markdowns also varies with different lines of merchandise, different months, and different seasons. The planned markdown figure is usually based on a normal amount determined from experience.

Step 1: Set the total markdown amount (stated as a percentage of total season's sales) for the entire period by:

(a) Reviewing and analyzing past markdown performance for the same period and for the entire period under consideration.

(b) Considering factors that may effect a change in markdowns.

Step 2: Convert the planned markdown percentage of sales to a total rupee figure for the season.

Step 3: Apportion total rupee planned markdowns by month.

5.4.1 Solved Example

Last year, net sales for the season in the swimwear department were ₹ 1,00,000. The total amount of markdowns taken during the entire period totalled ₹ 5,000. The buyer, upon reviewing the performance of the department and in preparation for planning markdowns for the same period this year, decided the ₹ 5,000 markdown figure taken previously was normal and compared favourably with standard markdown percentages established for this type of merchandise. Consequently, last year's rupee markdown amount was converted to a percentage:

Markdowns 5,000/1,00,000 = 5%

The total planned sales figure established by the buyer for the season under consideration was set at ₹ 1,10,000. Because a repetition of the percentage of markdowns was desired for the forthcoming season, the rupee amount of markdowns to be taken was determined by:

1,10,000 Planned sales × 5% Planned markdowns = 5,500 Planned total markdown for the season

The amount of 5,500 would then be apportioned by rupee s to the individual months of the period.

5.4.2 Planning Markups

The buyer will have to constantly manipulate the actual markup to date in relation to the markup on additional purchases for the season to obtain the planned seasonal markup percentage. To "protect" profitability, the gross profit figure, including an estimated shortage amount, can be calculated.

5.4.2.1 Solved Example

(1) For the Spring season, a department has planned:

- Sales @ ₹ 20,00,000
- Markdowns @ ₹ 2,00,000 (10%)
- Shortages @ ₹ 40,000 (2%).

(2) The department came into the period under consideration with an opening inventory at retail of ₹ 5,00,000, and a cumulative markup for the period of 52%.

(3) A closing inventory of ₹ 5,00,000 at retail is projected for the end of the Spring period.

(4) Management projects a desired gross margin of 48.5% for the Spring period.

(5) Based on a 48.5% gross margin, the cumulative markup (stock + purchases) is calculated:

Cumulative MU% = 48.5% GM + 12% Red (10% MDs + 2% SH)/(100% Sales + 12% Reductions) = 60.5/112 = 54%

(6) The markup percentage required on new purchases to meet desired goals is determined by the following method:

		Retails	Cost	Markup%
Net Sales	20,00,000			
Markdowns	2,00,00			
Shortages	40,000			
Closing inventory	5,00,000			
Total		27,40,000	27,40,000* 46% = 12,60,400	54%
Opening inventory		–5,00,000	–2,40,000	52%
New purchases		22,40,000	10,20,400	54.4%#

Markup on new purchases 22,40,000 – 10,20,400 = 12,19,600

Markup % = 12,19,600/22,40,000 = 54.4%

Further explanation:

Rupee sales (from plan) = ₹ 20,00,000

Rupee markdown (from plan) (10%) = 2,00,000

Anticipated rupee shortage = 40,000

Shortage % × Total planned rupee sales = ₹ 40,000 (2% × 20,00,000)

Planned Markup % on stock + Purchases = 54.0%

Cost or complement % on planned stock + Purchases = 46.0%

Cost of planned sales:

Planned markdown = ₹ 2,00,000 × 46% = ₹ 92,000

Planned shortage = 40,000 × 46% = 18,400

Planned sales = ₹ 20,00,000 × 46% = + 9,20,000

Total = ₹ 10,30,400

Planned rupee sales = ₹ 20,00,000

Cost of planned sales = –10,30,400

Planned ₹ gross profit – ₹ 9,69,600

Planned gross profit

= ₹ 9,69,600/20,00,000 = 48.5%

Planned Purchases—Planned Receipts

One objective of planning is to assist the buyer in proper timing and in purchasing the correct amounts of goods. Therefore, when the planned sales, stocks, and markdowns have been determined, the amount of monthly purchases is automatically calculated by a formula. Planned purchases, which is more accurately termed planned receipts, refers to the rupee amount of merchandise that can be brought into stock during a given period.

5.4.2.2 Solved Example

From the following planned figures for the lingerie department, calculate the planned purchase amount for June:

Planned stock June 1 = ₹ 38,000

Planned sales for June = ₹ 1,00,000

Planned markdowns for June = 5,000

Planned stock for July1 = 40,000

Solution:

Planned June sales ₹ 1,00,000

+ Planned EOM stock (July 1) 40,000

+ Planned June markdowns + 5,000

Total merchandise requirements = ₹ 1,45,000

– Planned BOM stock (June 1) – 38,000

Planned monthly retail purchases = ₹ 1,07,000

Converting Retail Planned Purchases to Cost

The planned purchase figure at retail must be established first before the planned purchase figure at cost is determined by conversion.

Planned purchase at cost = Planned retail purchases (R) × (100% – markup MU%)

5.4.2.3 Solved Example

The planned retail purchases for June were ₹ 1,07,000, and the planned MU% was 41.5%. Calculate the planned purchase amount at cost.

Solution:

Planned purchases = ₹ 1,07,000 × (100% – 41.5%)

= ₹ 1,07,000 × 58.5%

= ₹ 62,595

Planned Purchases at Cost = ₹ 62,595

5.5 OPEN TO BUY CONTROL

Merchandise control results from effective use of data that is available through the rupee planning procedure. In purchasing merchandise, a buyer is guided by the timing and quantity goals established in the six month seasonal rupee plan. To provide an even tighter control on the amount of merchandise received in a specific period and to achieve as precisely as possible the sales and stock plans, the buyer refers to a merchandising figure called OPEN-TO-BUY. This term, abbreviated OTB, denotes the amount of unspent (i.e., order limit) money that is available for purchasing merchandise that will be delivered during a given period. Usually, it is calculated on a monthly basis and indicates that the buyer has not yet spent all of the planned purchases or receipts for the period in question. It represents the difference between the planned purchases for a period and the merchandise orders already placed for that period. Unfilled orders, generally known as open orders, or "on order," should be charged to those months during which delivery is expected so that the buyer is able to control and time buying activities to correlate with selling activities. The purpose of this control is to identify the deviations between actual results and planned goals and so the buyer can take corrective measures when needed.

The planned purchase figure for a particular month indicates the sum available to purchase goods during the month, but this figure does not indicate the distribution of the money throughout the month. Experienced buyers attempt to distribute purchases over the entire month to:

- Reorder or replace fast selling goods.
- Fill in stocks so that complete stocks are offered.
- Compete advantageously when buying special purchases and/or new and interesting items as they become available.
- Test offerings of new resources.

Calculating Retail Open-to-Buy at the Beginning of a Month

OTB: Planned purchases for the month minus outstanding orders to be delivered that month

5.5.1 Solved Example

A buyer has planned January sales of ₹ 60,000, with an opening January stock planned at ₹ 50,000, a closing stock of ₹ 30,000, and markdowns planned at ₹ 500. If the orders that have already been placed for January delivery amount to ₹ 10,000 at retail, what is the buyer's January open-to-buy?

Solution:

January EOM stock + January sales + January markdowns =

₹ 30,000 + 60,000 + 500

Total merchandise requirements = 90,500

January BOM stock = –50,000

January planned purchases = ₹ 40,500

January on order = –10,000

January OTB at retail = ₹ 30,500

When the retail open-to-buy for any period is established, it can be converted to a cost open-to-buy figure. For example, ₹ 30,500 retail open-to-buy is converted to a cost figure by multiplying the retail open-to-buy by 100% (minus the planned markup percentage).

OTB for Balance of Month Based on Predetermined Planned Purchases

OTB for balance of month = Planned purchases for month – Merchandise received to day – On order = Open-to-buy

5.5.2 Solved Example

The merchandise plan shows that the planned purchases for September amounts to ₹ 17,000. The store's records indicate that from September 1 to September 15 the department received ₹ 8,300 worth of new goods and there is an order of ₹ 700 for September delivery. What is the open-to-buy for the balance of the month?

Solution:

September planned purchases	= ₹ 17,000
– Merchandise received	– 8,300
– On order	– 700
September OTB balance	₹ 8,000

OTB for Balance of Month Based on Planned Closing Stock

∴ OTB for balance of month

= Planned EOM stock + Planned sales for balance of month + Planned markdowns for balance of month

= Total merchandise requirements – Actual stock on hand – On order

= OTB for balance of the month

5.5.3 Solved Example

On September 15, an infants' department has a stock of ₹ 26,000 and merchandise on order amounting to ₹ 700. The planned sales for the balance of September are ₹ 8,000, with planned markdowns for the balance of the month at ₹ 500. The stock planned for September 30 is ₹ 31,800. What is the OTB for the balance of the month?

Solution:

Planned sales for balance of month ₹ 8,000

+ Planned markdowns for balance of month + 500

+ Planned EOM stock + 31,800

Total merchandise requirements = 40,300

– Actual stock on hand = –26,000

– On order = –700

September OTB balance = ₹ 13,600

5.6 PROBLEMS FOR PRACTICE

1. The coat department's net sales were ₹ 2,25,000, markdowns taken amounted to ₹ 15,000, and employee discounts were ₹ 3,000. The retail opening inventory for this period was ₹ 75,000, the purchases made at retail were ₹ 2,10,000, and the buyer estimated the shortages at 296. Determine the estimated physical count.

2. A store with net sales of ₹ 35,00,000 has estimated its shortages to be 2%. The actual rupee shortage amounted to ₹ 72,000.

   (a) Was this shortage a higher or lower percentage than anticipated? By how much?

   (b) What was the difference between the estimated and the actual shortage?

3. In the children's department, the August sales were planned at ₹ 2,47,500 because of additional promotional events. The actual sales for this month last year were ₹ 2,25,000. What is the percentage increase in planned sales for August of this year?

4. During the month of August, sales for a sporting goods store are planned at ₹ 9,00,000, which is 15% of the planned season's total sales. Calculate the monthly sales for the balance of the season, if sales are planned as follows:

August:	5%	November:	18%
September:	14%	December:	25%
October:	16%	January:	12%

5. A small retailer is planning a 10% reduction in sales due to competition from major new department store. If last year's sales were ₹ 5,00,000, what sales figures should be planned for this year?

6. After a detailed analysis of sales by classification, the hosiery buyer determined a decline in the kneehi category. Last year's sales for this category were ₹ 75,000. This year the sales for this classification are planned at ₹ 60,000. What is the percentage of sales decline?

7. For the year, a shoe department has net sales of ₹ 25,00,000. The average stock carried during this period was ₹ 10,00,000. What was the annual rate of stock turn?

8. What is the open-to-buy for a department that has planned purchases of ₹ 71,500 and outstanding orders of ₹ 74,000?

9. The actual stock on April 1 is ₹ 1,16,000 with "on order" in April amounting to ₹ 18,000. Sales are planned at ₹ 75,000, with markdowns estimated to be 3.5%, and the stock on April 30 planned at ₹ 1,12,000. What is the OTB for this month?

10. On March 13, stock on hand is ₹ 16,300, with planned sales for the balance of the month at ₹ 9,000. Merchandise on order comes to ₹ 3,000 and the planned April 1 stock is ₹ 10,000. Find the balance of the OTB for March.

11. The May portion of a six month plan for a shop is as follows:

    Planned May sales = ₹ 37,500

    Planned May markdowns = 10%

    Planned May BOM stock = 66,000

    Planned June BOM stock = 59,000

    Planned markup = 49%

    (a) What are the planned May purchases at retail?

    (b) On May 1, the buyer is notified that ₹ 8,000 worth of goods (retail value) is on order. What is the open-to-buy at cost for May?

12. Find the OTB balance for December when on December 10 the stock on hand is ₹ 2,65,000 and the planned sales for the balance of the month are ₹ 1,71,000. Markdowns are planned at ₹ 11,000, planned inventory for December 31 is ₹ 1,50,000, with outstanding orders totalling ₹ 71,500.

13. March figures for a shoe department are:

Planned sales	₹ 5,10,000
Planned markdowns	6,000
Planned March 1 stock	9,06,000
Planned April 1 stock	6,30,000
Outstanding March orders	1,26,000
Planned markup	52%

    Calculate:

    (a) The planned March purchases at retail.

    (b) The March open-to-buy at cost.

14. A junior sportswear buyer was shown the following data:

    Planned sales ₹ 22,000

    BOM stock June 44,000

    BOM stock July 40,000

    Planned June markdown 1,000

    Find:

    (a) The OTB at retail, if "on order" for June delivery is ₹ 16,000 at retail.

    (b) The OTB at cost, if the planned markup is 56%.

15. In a junior dress department, planned sales for the six month period February through July were ₹ 2,50,000. The monthly inventories at retail for this period were:

Dates	Stock on hand
February 1	₹ 90,000
March 1	87,000
April 1	92,000
May 1	90,000
June 1	84,000
July 1	79,000
July 31	62,000
Total	₹ 5,84,000

(a) What is the planned average stock for the period?

(b) What is the planned annual turnover based on the performance of this six month period?

(c) If planned sales in April were ₹ 23,000, what is the stock sales ratio for April?

16. For the Fall season, a boutique with a 3.0 turnover has planned the following sales:

August	₹ 1,00,700	November	₹ 1,16,900
September	1,13,500	December	1,18,200
October	1,50,000	January	1,00,000

Using the basic stock method, find the BOM **stock figures for each month**

17. Consider the following figures:

	BOM stocks	Net sales
January	₹ 50,000	₹ 15,000
February	46,000	18,000
March	46,000	20,000
April	46,000	14,000
May	40,000	12,000
June	40,000	16,000
July	45,000	14,000
August	45,000	14,000
September	50,000	18,000
October	60,000	18,000

November	80,000	38,000
December	44,000	16,000
January (following year)	46,000	

Find : (a) The yearly average stock figure.

(b) The turnover for the year.

(c) The turnover for September.

(d) The stock sales ratio for June.

18. The statistical division provides an accessories buyer with the following computerized information:

Planned sales for balance of month ₹ 1,62,000

Planned markdowns for balance of month 4,000

Planned EOM stock 2,00,000

Merchandise on order this month 64,000

Stock figure this date 2,14,000

Determine the balance of the month OTB.

5.7 ACTIVITY

Open a dummy shop. Start with 5 dummy products. Plan purchases, inventory, markup sales and profits. Assume your fixed costs are ₹ 50,000 per month. Plan your business on excel sheet.

CHAPTER 6

Invoice Mathematics

6.1 LEARNING OBJECTIVES

1. Traders use many methods to sell their goods, discounts, trade discounts are very important, you will learn
2. There many methods of credits. You will learn how sell goods on credits and relate discounts with credits.

6.2 DISCOUNTS

Goods move from a manufacturer to the ultimate consumer through the distribution chain or merchandising chain as mentioned below

Manufacturer

↓

Distributor

↓

Wholesaler

↓

Retailer

↓

Consumer

In the chain, a product is first sold by a manufacturer to one or more distributors. The agreement between a manufacturer and a distributor usually gives the distributor the exclusive right to distribute the product in a fairly large geographic region. The manufacturer sometimes prohibits the distributor from handling competing products. Typically, a distributor also has marketing responsibilities in the region. The distributor then resells the goods to a number of wholesalers. A wholesaler carries a wider range of products within a general category or theme. The majority of a wholesaler's product lines are complementary, but some will be competing. All are for resale to retailers within a smaller geographic area. Retailers sell mainly to the ultimate consumers of the goods.

In many cases, one or more of the intermediate links may be absent. Large national retailers and buying groups of smaller retailers may have enough buying power to purchase directly from manufacturers. To understand how prices are usually established within the merchandising chain, imagine that you are a wholesaler buying from a distributor. The distributor is likely to have a catalogue of list prices. List prices are commonly chosen to approximate the ultimate retail selling price. There are usual terms such as "manufacturer's suggested retail price," "suggested list price," or "recommended selling price" on the packaging or in advertisements

The distributor sometimes offers a percent discount from the list price called the trade discount rate. The word "trade" signifies that the discount applies only to a transaction within the "trade," that is, within the merchandising chain (but not including the consumer). There may be some negotiating room for setting the rate of trade discount.

"Trade discount" can refer to either the percent amount or the rupee amount of the discount. The intended meaning is sometimes obvious from the units quoted (% or Re). The "amount of the trade discount" will refer to the trade discount measured in rupees. For example, if a trade discount rate of 35% applies to a ₹ 200 list price item, the amount of the trade discount is 0.35 (₹ 200) = ₹ 70.

Billed cost = List price – Trade discounts

The resulting price after deducting the amount of the trade discount from the list price is called the net price. That is,

Net price = List price – Amount of trade discount

$N = L - L*d$

$N = L(1-d)$

Where N is Net price, L is List price, d = Rate of trade discount

Multiple Discounts (or Series Discounts)

In the past, it was common for a seller/vendor in the merchandising chain to offer more than one discount. For example, in addition to the basic trade discount offered to all customers, the seller might also offer small discounts for large volume purchases, for special promotions and cooperative advertising, and for early orders of seasonal items. If a purchaser qualifies for more than one discount, the understanding is that the discounts should be compounded rather than added.

This means that same formula can used but multiply with (1 – d) factor for each discount. If there are three discounts, d_1, d_2, and d_3, then the net price is

Net price after three discounts = $N = L(1 - d_1)(1 - d_2)(1 - d_3)$

The granting of separate multiple discounts has been largely abandoned. It is now much more typical for buyers and sellers to negotiate a single discount rate that can be adjusted

The use of trade discounts in conjunction with fixed list prices makes it easier for the seller to set different prices for various categories of customers. For example, a manufacturer might offer one discount rate to a distributor in one part of the country, another discount rate to "big-box" retailers, and yet another rate to smaller buying groups. Every customer sees the same "up front" list price. Price flexibility is achieved in the setting of the trade discount rate.

Over time as the business relationship evolves, rather than offering a volume discount on individual orders, vendors increasingly pay end of year discounts (in the 2% to 5% range) based on the cumulative volume of a customer's purchases during the year.

Single Discount Rate Equivalent to Multiple Discounts

An equivalent discount rate is the single discount rate that gives the same net price as the combined effect of the multiple discounts. Suppose, for example, that the net amount after applying three discounts to a list price of ₹ 100 is ₹ 75. Then the rupee amount of the discount is ₹ 100 – ₹ 75 = ₹ 25, and the equivalent discount rate is ₹ 25.

Indeed, formula, $N = L(1 - d)$, applies to any situation in which an amount (L) is reduced by d per cent. Such applications include the calculation of the "sale" price after a percentage markdown, sales revenue net of commission, security prices after a percentage loss in value, and budget amounts after a percentage cut. Similarly, formula, $N = L(1 - d_1)(1 - d_2)(1 - d_3)$ may be employed in any situation where a beginning amount, L, undergoes a series of compound percent decreases. N represents the amount left after the decreases. For example, suppose a product's sales are forecast to decline from the past year's sales of ₹ 2,00,000 by 10%, 20%, and 15% in successive years. Then sales in the third year are forecast to be N ₹ 2,00,000(1 – 0.10) (1 – 0.20)(1 – 0.15) = ₹ 2,00,000(0.90)(0.80)(0.85) = ₹ 1,22,400

Note that the three decreases result in an overall sales reduction of 38.8%. This is less than the sum (10% + 20% + 15% = 45%) of the three percentage decreases.

6.2.1 Solved Examples on Discounts

After a trade discount of 30%, an auto mechanic is able to purchase windshield wiper blades for a net price of ₹ 19.46. What is the list price of the blades?

Solution:

Given: d = 0.30, N = ₹ 19.46.

The list price of the blades is L = N/(1 – d) = 19.46/(1 – 0.30) = ₹ 27.80

6.2.2 Solved Example

XXX Manufacturing and Lace Clothing both produce basic work shirts that are very similar in quality and popularity. Both manufacturers quote a list price of ₹ 29.90 for the shirt. XXX offers a regular trade discount of 25% plus an additional volume discount of 10% on orders of at least 1,000 shirts. Lace offers a standard discount of 30% and a further 5% discount on orders exceeding 500 shirts. Which source will give the lower net price on an order for 1,000 shirts?

Solution:

Given: For XXX, L = 29.90, d_1 = 25%, d_2 = 10%, For Lace, L = 29.90, d_1 = 30%, d_2 = 5%. The net price per shirt from XXX is

$$N = L(1 - d_1)(1 - d_2) = 29.90(1 - 0.25)(1 - 0.10) = 29.90(0.75)(0.90) = 20.18$$

The net price per shirt from Lace Clothing is

$$N = L(1 - d_1)(1 - d_2) = 29.90(1 - 0.30)(1 - 0.05) = 29.90(0.70)(0.95) = 19.88$$

Therefore, Lace's net price is 30 per cents shirt lower. (Note that the sum of the two discount rates in each case is 35%. However, they do not have the same effect.)

6.2.3 Solved Example

Trade discounts on a lawnmower that "lists" as ₹ 200 are 25%, 10%, 5%. Find the billed cost on an item quoted at ₹ 200 list, less 25%, 10%, and 5%.

Solution:

List price = ₹ 200

Less 25% ₹ 200.00 – 50.00 (= 200 × 25%) = 1st discount

₹ 150.00 (resultant figure)

Less 10% ₹ 150.00 – 15.00 ($150 × 10%) = 2nd discount

₹ 135.00 (resultant figure)

Less 5% ₹ 135.00

–6.75 ($135 × 5%) = 3rd discount

₹ 128.25 (resultant figure)

Billed cost = ₹ 128.25

6.3 TERMS OF SALE

Cash Discounts and Terms of Payment

Other than the final sale to the consumer, transactions within the merchandising chain commonly involve "trade credit." Under this arrangement, the vendor does not require payment for goods during a "credit period" that can range from 15 days to a few weeks. No interest is charged during this interval. Following a transaction, the vendor sends the buyer an invoice, such as the sample shown below. The invoice presents details of the "terms of pay-

Bhagat Ram Gopal Das Supplier and Distributers
Crawford Wholesale Market, Bhandup, Mumbai

Sold to		
Chela Ram & Sons	Date: 17-7-2008	Invoice No. 3333
Crawford Retail Market,	Terms 2/10, n30	Via Chalta Firta Logistics
Nashik (Branch)		

Quantity	Product Number	Description	Unit List price	Discount	Net Ammount
5	K-31	Ex-Machine	₹ 2,300	30%	8050
150	T-4	Pulleys	₹ 56	25%, 15%	5355
1000	M-8a	Tread parts	₹ 2.20	35%, 10%, 7%	1196.91

Invoice Total = 14,601.91
Sales Tax = 2,190.29
Shipping Charges = 546.00
TOTAL AMOUNT DUE = ₹ 17,338.20

1.5% per month on overdue amount

E&OE

Quantity Discount

Quantity discount (QD) is a percentage off the billed cost given by a vendor when a stipulated quantity is purchased and is deductible regardless of when invoices are paid. Usually the purchase of a large amount of goods is involved. Although quantity discounts are not customary practice in the fashion industries, they are common in home furnishings and hard goods lines. Depending on custom and practice within individual industries, this kind of discount is offered either when the stipulated quantity is purchased, or it is given for accumulated purchases over a specified period of time. The amount of discount is based on a sliding scale (i.e., the larger the purchase, the greater the percentage of quantity discount). A quantity discount is offered as an incentive for buyers to commit to purchase large amounts of goods. Additionally, it is the buyer's responsibility to judge the merits of savings through this quantity discount against the risks of tying up more than the normal planned amounts of open-to-buy money.

6.3.1 Solved Example

A cookware manufacturer's established price schedule is:

- A minimum initial order of ₹ 500 receives a 1% QD.
- An initial order of ₹ 1,250 receives 1.5%.
- An initial order of ₹ 2,500 receives 2%, and so on.

On an order of assorted cookware amounting to ₹ 2,000, use this discount schedule to determine:

(a) The quantity discount.

(b) The net cost of this order.

Solution:

(a) Quantity discount = ₹ 2,000 Billed cost × 1.5% Quantity discount

= ₹ 30

(b) Billed cost (= ₹ 2,000)

– Quantity discount – 30

Net cost = ₹ 1,970

Cash discount, the most common kind of discount, is a stated percentage of the billed cost allowed by a vendor if payment of the invoice amount is made within a stipulated time. The full utilization of cash discounts is another approach to decreasing the total cost of merchandise that results in an increased profit potential. Although any invoice or bill must be paid within some specified time, the intent of the cash discount is to offer the purchaser an incentive to make early payment. The vendor sacrifices a fraction of the cost that is due to receive payment more rapidly. Cost prices that are subject to quantity and/or trade discounts may also be subject to cash discounts. Eligibility for a cash discount is contingent on the time element only. The cash discount percentage is not only written on the purchase order, but also on the vendor's invoice (e.g., 8/10 terms refers to an 896 discount if the invoice is paid within 10 days).

Calculating Net Cost when Billed Cost and Cash Discount are known

Concept:

Net cost = Billed cost − Cash discount

6.3.2 Solved Example

The cost of a microwave oven is ₹ 6,000. The cash discount earned is 6%. What is the net cost paid to the manufacturer?

Solution:

Cash discount = 6,000 Billed cost × 6% Cash discount

Cash discount = ₹ 360

Billed cost = 6,000

–Cash discount = –360

Net cost = 5,640 (Amount to be remitted)

Net cost = List price − Trade discount(s) − Cash discount

6.3.3 Solved Example

The list price of a lawnmower is ₹ 200 less 25%, less 10%, less 5%. There is a 2% discount offered for payment within ten days. What is the amount to be remitted if the cash discount is earned?

Solution

1St discount = 200*25% = 50

1st Price = 200 − 50 = 150

2nd discount = 150*10% = 15

2nd price = 150 – 15 = 135

3rd discount = 135*5% = 6.75

3rd Price = 135 − 6.75 = 128.25

Cash Discount = 128.25*2% = 2.57

Net price = 128.25 – 2.57 = ₹ 125.68

When the cost of goods for some types of merchandise is stated by quoting a list price with a series of discounts and the buyer is granted a quantity discount and is also eligible for a cash discount, the amount to be remitted to the vendor is calculated by:

- First, deducting the series of trade discounts to find the billed cost.
- Second, determining the eligibility for the quantity discounts offered and deducting the percentage of dollar amount from the calculated billed cost.
- Third, subtracting the cash discount from this amount.

6.4 DATING

The length of the credit period

The credit period is the length of time for which trade credit is granted. The invoice amount is due at the end of the credit period. Normally, interest is not charged for the credit period. It is common practice to charge a penalty on overdue amounts. The "1.5% per month" indicated on the sample invoice means that any portion of the invoice amount that goes overdue (anywhere from one day to one month) is liable for a 1.5% penalty. How strictly a vendor enforces the penalty is a judgment call.

The cash discount rate offered (if any) and the length of the discount period. A cash discount is a deduction allowed for prompt payment of the invoice amount (or any portion thereof). The time period within which a payment qualifies for the cash discount is called the discount period, the date on which both the credit period and the discount period begin. The most common system for presenting the terms of payment is known as ordinary dating or invoice dating.

With ordinary dating, both the credit period and the discount period are measured from the invoice date (day "0"). For example, if an invoice dated July 3 has a 30-day credit period, then July 4 is counted as "day 1," July 5 as "day 2," and so on. August 2 will be "Day 30," the final day of the credit period. A payment received on August 2 falls within the credit period, but a payment received on August 3 is liable for the overdue account penalty. A shorthand notation is normally used on an invoice to present the terms of payment. The abbreviation "2/10, n/30" is read as "two ten, net thirty."

Dating is an agreement between the supplier and retailer whereby a specified time period for payment of an invoice is arranged. Dating arrangements vary within any particular industry and from one industry to another. Dating usually implies a cash discount and is expressed as a single term of sale (e.g., 2/10). This means that the buyer will deduct a 2% cash discount from the billed cost if the payment is remitted to the manufacturer on or before the stipulated 10-day period.

For example, 2/10, net 30 means that a 2% discount off the billed cost is permitted if the invoice is paid within 10 days following the date of invoice. The payment of the net amount (i.e., total amount of billed cost) is required between the 11th and the 30th day following the date of the invoice.

6.4.1. Solved Example

An invoice, dated March 1, for 10 folding chairs at a cost of ₹ 24 each, carries terms of 2/10, net 30. If the bill is paid on any day from March 1 to March 11, 2% may be deducted. How much should be paid if the invoice is paid on March 8?

Solution:

Invoice amount = 24*10 – 24*10*2% = 235.25 rupees

However, if the bill is paid on or after March 12, the full amount of ₹ 240 is due.

6.4.2 Different Types of Dating

There are many different types of dating used in all industries. Variations can even occur within a particular industry. Generally, the nature of the goods influences the prevalent dating practices. For example, some segments of the apparel industry offer a relatively high cash discount (e.g., 8%) to induce purchasers to take advantage of the savings inherent for early or prompt payment. This is vital in an industry composed of many small businesses that are frequently undercapitalized. From the standpoint of the purchaser (i.e., retailer) who invokes the cash discount privileges, the cost of the merchandise is considerably reduced, which has potential implications for increased profits. In the determination of when to pay an invoice, the buyer must be able to distinguish between the discount date and the net payment date. The **discount date** is the date by which the invoice may be paid to take advantage of the discount granted, and the **net payment date** is the date by which the invoice must be paid to acquire a favourable credit rating and avoid possible late penalties.

When economic conditions are not favorable, a retailer may be prone to disregard or possibly extend the traditional negotiated time period. Under these conditions, the vendor usually makes exceptions and concentrates on invoice payment rather than the strict observance of datings. Nonetheless, the most important negotiation is to set a specific date for payment of an invoice, and then be able to calculate the exact payment date. Even though there are different numbers of days for each month throughout the year, to simplify the payment calculations, many businesses will base their calculations on a 30 day month. Many businesses who want to take advantage of all possible days in the payment period prefer using the traditional calendar. Since individual arrangements can vary, for the purpose of identification and the application of the various types of dating, the problems and illustrations used in this text calculate the discount and net payment dates on a 30 day month.

There are many types of dating

1. COD dating
2. Regular dating
3. Extra dating

4. EOM dating

5. ROG dating

COD Dating

COD dating (cash on delivery) is a type of dating that means payment must be made "on the spot" as delivery takes place. Generally, COD dating is applicable to purchasers with poor or unproven credit ratings.

6.4.3 Solved Example

Goods valued at ₹ 500 cost are purchased by a retail store under COD dating terms. What amount must be remitted? When?

Solution:

Invoice amount = ₹ 500; Amount remitted = ₹ 500 When = As delivery takes place

Regular (or Ordinary) Dating

Regular or ordinary dating is one of the most common kinds of dating. The discount period is calculated from the date of the invoice, which is usually the same date that the merchandise is shipped.

6.4.4 Solved Example

What payment should be made on an invoice for ₹ 500 dated November 16, carrying terms of 4/10, net 30?

Solution:

If paid on or before November 26 (November is 16 + 10 days)

Billed cost ₹ 500.00

– Cash discount (₹ 500 × 4%) – 20.00

Remitted = ₹ 500 – 20 = ₹ 480

If paid between November 27 and December 17 (i.e., 20 day net payment period), no discount is permitted, and the full ₹ 500 is remitted. The vendor reserves the right to charge carrying fees after the expiration of the net payment period. The exercising or bypassing of this option depends on individual cases (e.g., credit history, the relationship of the vendor to the retailer, etc.).

Extra Dating

Extra dating (written as an X) is calculated from the date of the invoice, with a specified number of extra days granted, during which the discount may be taken. Consequently, 2/10-60X means that the bill is payable in 10 days plus 60 extra days (i.e., a total of 70 days) from the date of the invoice to earn the 2% discount. The full amount is due after the expiration of the 70 days and the customary, though often unstated, 20 day additional net payment period follows.

6.4.5 Solved Example

An invoice dated March 16 has a billed cost of ₹ 1,800 and terms of 3/10-60X.

Determine:

(a) Final date for taking cash discount.

(b) Cash discount earned if bill is paid June 14.

(c) Amount due if paid in full on April 17.

(d) Last date for net payment.

Solution:

(a) Final date for cash discount: March 16 through 30 = 14 days April (entire month) = 30 days May 1 through 26 = 26 days

End of cash discount period = May 26 = 70 days Cash discount allowable through May 26 only.

(b) None

(c) Eligible for cash discount: ₹ 1,800 Billed cost – 54 (₹ 1,800 × 3% Cash discount)

₹ 1,746 Amount due

₹ 1,746 Amount due if paid in full on April 17.

(d) Last date for net payment:

20 days after May 26 = June 16

Last date for net payment: June 16.

EOM Dating

EOM dating (end of month) means the cash discount period is computed from the end of the month in which the invoice is dated rather than from the date of the invoice itself. Thus, 8/10 EOM (invoice dated April 1) means that the time for payment is calculated from the end of April, Additionally, an 8% cash discount may be taken if the bill is paid by May 10, that is, ten days after the end of April. Again a twenty day net period occurs from May 11 through May 31 (implied), during which the retailer may pay the bill in full.

(**Note:** Traditionally, under EOM dating only, invoices dated on or after the 25th of any month are considered to be part of the next month's transactions 2. For example, a bill with 8/10 EOM dated on August 26, is considered a September 1 bill and the discount period extends to October 10. Of course, arrangements of this kind vary).

6.4.6 Solved Example

An invoice for ₹ 1,000 dated March 17 has terms of 8/10 EOM.

(a) What is the last date for deducting 8% cash discount?

(b) What amount will be due if the bill is paid on that date?

Solution:

(a) Discount date = April 10 (ten days after end of March)

April 10 is the last date for 8% discount.

(b) ₹ 1,000 Billed cost

– 80 ($1,000 × 8% Cash discount)

₹ 920 Amount due

₹ 920 due if paid by April 10.

If this invoice was dated March 26 through to March 31 (using the traditional calendar), the discount date of payment would be May 10.

ROG Dating

ROG dating (receipt of goods) is when the discount period is calculated from the date the goods are delivered to the retailer's premises, rather than from the date of the invoice. This type of dating is often requested by buyers located at a considerable distance from the market (or shipping point). These retailers typically receive bills a few days after shipment, but may not get delivery of the merchandise itself for a considerably longer time. Therefore, 5/10 ROG, for example, means that the bill must be paid within 10 days after receipt of goods to earn the cash discount.

6.4.7 Solved Example

An invoice for ₹ 100 is dated April 4 and carries terms of 5/10 ROG. The goods arrive in the store on May 7.

(a) What is the last date that the discount may be deducted?

(b) How much should be remitted if payment is made on that date?

Solution:

(a) Date Goods Were Received + 10 days

May 7 + 10 days

= May 17

Last day for discount = May 17

(b) ₹ 100 Billed cost – ₹ 5 (₹ 100 × 5% Cash discount) = ₹ 95 amount due on or before May 17.

Advanced or Postdating

Advanced or postdating (seasonal discount) is the type of dating that indicates the invoice date is advanced so that additional time is allowed for payment to be made and, ultimately, for the cash discount to be deducted. The discount period is then calculated from this advanced date agreed upon by the buyer and the seller. Generally, this type of dating is used by manufacturers to persuade buyers to buy and/or receive goods earlier than they would normally. Also, it is requested by purchasers who are momentarily short of cash. Consequently, if a shipment was made on February 10 and the invoice date was May 1, terms of 2/10 would mean that payment was due on or before May 11 to qualify for a 2% cash discount. (Please note that on invoices with advance or postdating, the payment of the invoice, at net, is delayed until the last day of the month in which the cash discount is earned, after which it is considered overdue).

6.4.8 Solved Example

An invoice for merchandise shipped on August 18 is postdated October 1 and carries terms of 3/10, net 30. When does the discount period expire?

Solution:

3% may be deducted if payment is made on or before October 11. The full amount is due at the end of the customary net period on October 31, using the traditional calendar.

Interpreting the Terms of Payment in Ordinary Dating

2/10, n/30 means Cash discount (2%), Discount period (10 days) and Credit period (30 days). The 2% cash discount is credited on either partial payments or full payment made on or before the last day of the discount period. The balance is due by the end of the 30 day credit period. A variation of the ordinary dating notation is "2/10, 1/30, n/60." In this case, a reduced cash discount of 1% is offered on payments made any time from the eleventh to the thirtieth day after the invoice date. The following are common practices with ordinary dating (and with the two other notations described in the appendix). If the last day of the discount period or the credit period falls on a non business day, the period is extended to the next business day. If no cash discount is offered, only the "net" figure for the credit period is given (for example, n/15 or n/30). If a net figure for the credit period is not stated, it is understood that the credit period ends 20 days after the end of the discount period. For example, "2/10" by itself implies "2/10, n/30". Formula N = L (1 – d), may be used to calculate the amount required to settle an invoice if the cash discount is taken. Substitute the invoice amount for L and the cash discount rate for d. The value calculated for N is the full payment that will settle the invoice within the discount period. A partial payment is any payment smaller than the initial amount required to fully satisfy the invoice. Unless otherwise indicated on the invoice, partial payments made within the discount period are eligible for the cash discount. The basic discount formula may be used to calculate the amount credited to the customer's account.

6.4.9 Solved Example

An invoice for ₹ 1,079.80 with terms 2/10, n/30 is dated November 25. It was received in the mail on November 27. What payment will settle the invoice if payment is made on:

(a) December 1

(b) December 5 or

(c) December 7

Solution:

The last day of the discount period is the tenth day after the invoice date (November 25). November has 30 days. Therefore, payments made on or before December 5 are eligible for the 2% cash discount. The payment required to settle the invoice is: N = L (1 – d) = 1079.80 (1 – 0.02) = 1,058.20 After December 5, the full amount must be paid to settle the invoice. The payment required is ₹ 1,079.80.

6.4.10 Solved Example

Bajaj Electric received an invoice for ₹ 3845 dated March 25 with terms 3/10, 1/20, n/60. Roland paid ₹ 1,500 on April 4, ₹ 500 on April 12, and ₹ 500 on April 30. What balance was still owed after April 30?

Solution

The 3% discount applies to any payment made on or before April 4 (March 25, 10 days.) The 1% discount applies to any payment made in the period April 5 to April 14, inclusive. Therefore, the ₹ 1,500 payment qualifies for the 3% discount, and the first ₹ 500 payment qualifies for the 1% discount.

Amount credited = Amount paid/(1 – d)

Total of the credits for the first three payments is

1,500/(1 – 0.03) + 500/(1 – 0.01) + 500 = 1,546.39 + 505.05 + 500 = 2,551.44

Balance owed = 3,845 – 2,551.44 = 1,293.56

Activity

Determine the settlement amount on payment date in the following cases

Problem	Invoice Amount In	₹ Credit Term	Invoice Date	Payment Date
1	2,365	2/10,n/30	Sept 25	Oct 5
2	2,365	1.5/15,n/45	Oct 25	Nov 10
3	815.49	2/10,1/20,n/60	June 27	July 7
4	5,445	3/10,1.5/20,n/60	March 23	April 13

6.5 ANTICIPATION

Anticipation is an extra discount, which is usually calculated at the prevailing prime rate of business interest and is subject to change based on economic conditions. This extra discount is often permitted by vendors when an invoice is paid prior to the end of the cash discount period and, again, is subject to change based on economic conditions. For the purpose of illustration only, this text will use a 6% annual rate, which equates to 0.5% per month, or a decimal equivalent of .005 per month.

The number of days of anticipation is based upon the number of days remaining between the actual date of payment of an invoice and the last date on which the cash discount could be taken. While some vendors do not permit an anticipation discount, alert retailers deduct it, unless a notation on the invoice expressly forbids it. Many retailers, when sending in a confirmed order, specify "anticipation allowed." Anticipation is taken by retailers because, in effect, the vendor has the use of the retailer's money ahead of the date arranged by the terms of the sale, and because of this the retailer is charging the vendor "interest" for its use. An anticipation deduction is taken in addition to any other discounts that may apply, and the deduction percentage customarily is combined with the regular cash discount percentage.

Currently, however, some retailers are anticipating invoices based on the number of days from the date of payment to the end of the net period. When using this policy, a bill that is paid after the cash discount period has ended can still be anticipated for the balance of the net period.

6.5.1 Solved Example

An invoice for ₹ 100 is dated December 4 and carries terms of 2/10-30X. Anticipation is permitted. If the bill is paid on December 14:

(a) Calculate the number of days that were anticipated and the remittance due using the cash discount period method.

(b) Determine the number of days that were anticipated and the remittance due using the net payment period method.

Solution:

(a) Using the traditional cash discount period method.

The cash discount period is 40 days.

Because the bill is paid in 10 days the anticipation period is 30 days.

Total rupee amount of goods = ₹ 100

Anticipation = .5% for 30 days

Cash discount = 2%

Cash discount + anticipation = 2% + .5% = 2.5%

Total discount = ₹ 100 × 2.5% = 2.50

Net cost = 100 – ₹ 2.50 = ₹ 97.50

Amount remitted = ₹ 97.50

(b) Using the net payment period method or an alternate approach to anticipation.

The cash discount period is 40 days and the net payment period is 60 days. Because the bill is paid in 10 days, the anticipation period is 50 days.

(**Note:** Using the net payment period method, if this invoice was paid after 40 days, that is, after the cash discount period had elapsed, the buyer would still be allowed an anticipation discount for the 20 days remaining in the net payment period.)

Total rupee amount of goods = 100

Anticipation = .82% for 50 days

Cash discount = 2%

Cash discount + anticipation = 2% + .82% +

Total discount = ₹ 100 × 2.82% = ₹ 2.82

Net cost = 100 – ₹ 2.82 = $97.18

Amount remitted ₹ 97.18

6.6 LOADING

Loading is the practice of intentionally increasing the amount of the invoice to a price that would allow a theoretically greater cost discount, but results in paying the net amount that the vendor quotes. The standardized cash discount percentage arbitrarily set by top management does not reflect the true cash discount allowed by the vendor. When loading is practiced, the retailer may request the vendor to bill a "loaded" cost that is then adjusted by the required cash discount percentage to achieve the true net cost. In other cases, the store will make the adjustment statistically when the invoices are processed.

6.6.1 Solved Example

A manufacturer quotes the cost of an item at ₹ 30 with terms of 3/10, n/30. The buyer desired an 8% cash discount. What is the "loaded" cost?

Solution:

Net cost of invoice = ₹ 30 Billed cost – 3% Cash discount = ₹ 29.10

Loaded cost = 29.10/ (100 – 8%) = ₹ 31.63

6.7 PROBLEMS FOR PRACTICE

1. The Robner Electronic Company lists a top of the line answering machine for ₹ 175. The trade discount offered is 30%. What is the billing price?
2. A guitar manufacturer sells electric guitars at ₹ 450 less 30% and 10%. What is the net cost to the buyer?
3. Dealer A sells stereo sets for ₹ 975 with a 30% trade discount. Competitor B offers a similar model at ₹ 760 with a 15% discount. Which is the better buy? By how much?
4. If a buyer purchases 120 coats at ₹ 52 each and earns an 8% cash discount, what amount must be paid to the manufacturer?
5. A gift store received an invoice in the amount of ₹ 8,200, which represents the manufacturer's suggested retail price. The invoice also shows that a trade discount of 45% is allowed, as well as a 2% cash discount. Determine the amount of payment to the vendor.
6. A sporting goods buyer purchased 50 individual golf clubs of one style that cost ₹ 35 each. When the merchandise was received, the invoice indicated that an additional 5% quantity discount was allowed when more than 36 clubs of any one style were purchased. Additionally, a 3% cash discount was allowed when payment was made within 10 days. What amount should have been remitted to the manufacturer if payment was made in 7 days?
7. The housewares department placed an order for two dozen food processors that have a list price of ₹ 300 each, with trade discounts of 30%, 10%, and 5%. The supplier's price schedule is:

- A minimum order of ₹ 3,000: 1%.
- An initial order of ₹ 4,000: 1.5%.
- An initial order of ₹ 5,000: 2%.
- Payments within 10 days: 2% cash discount.

If this invoice was paid in nine days, what amount should have been remitted to the seller?

8. A retailer has in stock a microcomputer that lists for ₹ 1,950. Trade discounts of 35% and 10% were quoted.

   (a) What is the billed cost?

   (b) At what price would the microcomputer sell if the retailer decided to apply a 48% markup?

9. If you were a buyer with an invoice that came to a list price of ₹ 100, which set of series trade discounts would you favor?

   (a) 25%, 20%, and 15%,

   or

   (b) 50% and 10% Explain your choice.

10. Your department receives an invoice dated October 10 in the amount of ₹ 6,750. How much must be paid on November 10 if terms are:

    (a) 10/10, net 30.

    (b) 10/10 EOM.

    (c) Net.

11. Merchandise that amounts to ₹ 650 at cost is shipped and invoiced on August 14. Terms are 4/10 EOM. Payment is made on August 26. How much should be remitted?

12. A buyer purchased 75 ginger jar lamps at a list price of ₹ 40 each. The trade discounts were 30%, 20%, and 5% with terms of 2/10, net 30. The lamps were shipped and billed on October 18 and were received October 22. The bill was paid on October 31. What amount was paid?

13. An invoice dated March 2 carries terms of 3/10-60X. When does the discount period expire? Explain.

14. Goods are invoiced and shipped on July 1 and received on July 15. Terms are 5/10 EOM and the invoice is for ₹ 5,600. Payment is made on August 10. How much should be remitted?

15. An invoice for ₹ 3,290, dated April 26th, covering merchandise received May 19th, carries terms of 8/10 EOM, ROG. It is paid on June 10.

    (a) How much should have been remitted?

    (b) What would have been remitted had ROG not been included? Why?

16. Goods that are invoiced on July 26 are received on August 10. Indicate the final discount date for net payment and the final date for net payment if terms are:

	Final discount date	Net payment date
(a) 3/10 EOM	________	________
(b) 2/10, net 30	________	________
(c) 1/20-30x	________	________
(d) 8/10 EOM as of Sept. 1	________	________
(e) 8/10 EOM, ROG	________	________

17. On June 24, a buyer received a purchase that amounted to a total list price of ₹ 16,000. This merchandise had a trade discount of 37.5%. The buyer wanted to negotiate with the supplier the last date possible to take a cash discount. The invoice on this purchase was dated June 22. Determine the various cash payment dates for the buyer under the following purchase terms:

    (a) 2/10, n/30.

    (b) 2/10, n/30 ROG.

    (c) 2/10, n/30 EOM.

    (d) 2/10-60X, anticipation allowed.

6.8 ACTIVITY

Interview 10 wholesalers and distributors of FMCG and ask various schemes and discounts and write a report.

CHAPTER 7

Computing by Heart

7.1 LEARNING OBJECTIVES

After going through this chapter, you will learn

(a) Introduction to Vedic mathematics

(b) Simple calculations by heart

(c) Trade calculations by heart

7.2 HOW WE CALCULATE

Indian management system is unique. Indian managers are recognised all over the world for better management, human relations, planning, communication and coordination. Their thought process is human than mechanical. Indian retailers never depended on computing machines, thanks to pedagogy at primary education level. Our inbuilt system of Vedic mathematics make us experts in additions, subtraction, multiplication. The book 'Vedic Mathematics' by Sri Bharti Krishna Tirthaji clearly shows how advanced were our forefathers in computing difficult propositions of arithmetic, algebra and geometry. If the basic numbers are understood, the whole subject of Math can be developed without any external help. Numbers are totally reliable and dependable. Unlike human beings, they always behave in the same way.

The benefits of using Vedic Math are many:

- It will increase your mental agility.
- It will improve your memory.

- It will give you more confidence.
- You will gain the ability to make quick calculations: in the shop, at work, on the phone, etc.

The Vedic system is **completely natural**. It works the way your mind works.

The examples used are taken from Vedic mathematics text and also from the authors who further translated to their practical uses.

There are sixteen sutras. Only two/three sutra are explained which can be used by retailers for their benefits. The purpose is to avoid calculators. It has been observed that present generation is becoming slave of machines like calculators and computers. We encourage simple mental calculations.

For example, in order to subtract 23 from 55, you would probably set the numbers out one below the other and use the subtraction method you have been taught (one of the two main methods currently in education). But stop and study these numbers briefly. Notice that 23 is 3 above 20. So, simply take 20 from 55 (which gives 35) and subtract 3 back to get 32. Thus, 55 – 23 = 32. Such a process is more in tune with our natural thinking processes than the traditional, formal steps we learn in western system. We do not say

Multiplication

Using VERTICALLY AND CROSSWISE,

Suppose you need 9 × 6

9 is 1 below 10 and 6 is 4 below 10.

Think of it like this:

91

64

54

The answer is 54.

You subtract crosswise 9 – 4 or 6 – 1 to get 5, the first figure of the answer.

And you multiply vertically: 4 × 1 to get 4, the last figure of the answer.

See how far the numbers are below 10, subtract one number's deficiency from the other number, and multiply the deficiencies together.

- **7 × 6 = 42**

```
7   3
  ×
6   4
3  12  = 42
```

Here there is a carry: the 1 in the 12 goes over to make 3 into 4.

Here's how to use VERTICALLY AND CROSSWISE for multiplying numbers close to 100.

- Suppose you want to **multiply 88 by 98.**

Not easy, you might think. But with

VERTICALLY AND CROSSWISE you can give the answer immediately, using the same method as above.

Both 88 and 98 are close to 100.

88 is 12 below 100 and 98 is 2 below 100.

You can imagine the sum set out like this:

```
88 - 12
   ×
98 -  2
86   24
```

As before the **86** comes from subtracting crosswise: 88 − 2 = 86 (or 98 − 12 = 86: you can subtract either way, you will always get the same answer). And the **24** in the answer is just 12 × 2: you multiply vertically. So **88 × 98 = 8,624**

Multiplying numbers just over 100

• **103 × 104 = 10,712**

The answer is in two parts: 107 and 12,

107 is just 103 + 4 (or 104 + 3), and 12 is just 3 × 4.

• Similarly **107 × 106 = 11,342**

107 + 6 = 113 and 7 × 6 = 42

How we find square of a number ending 5

A quick way to square numbers that end in 5 using the formula BY ONE MORE THAN THE ONE BEFORE.

• **75^2 = 5,625**

75^2 means 75 × 75.

The answer is in two parts: 56 and 25.

The last part is always **25.**

The first part is the first number, 7, multiplied by the number "one more", which is 8:

so 7 × 8 = **56**

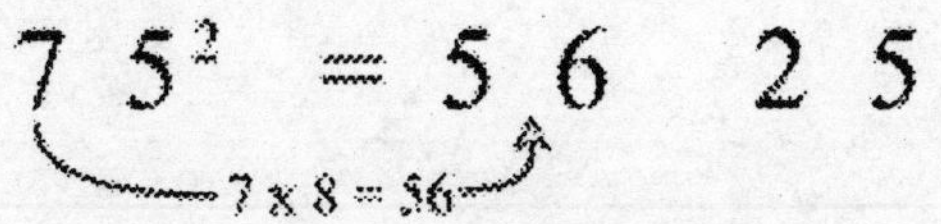

• Similarly **85^2 = 7,225** because 8 × 9 = 72.

Method for multiplying numbers where the first figures are the same and the last figures add up to 10.

• **32 × 38 = 1,216**

Both numbers here start with 3 and the last figures (2 and 8) add up to 10.

So we just multiply 3 by 4 (the next number up) to get **12** for the first part of the answer.

And we multiply the last figures: 2 × 8 = **16** to get the last part of the answer.

Diagrammatically:

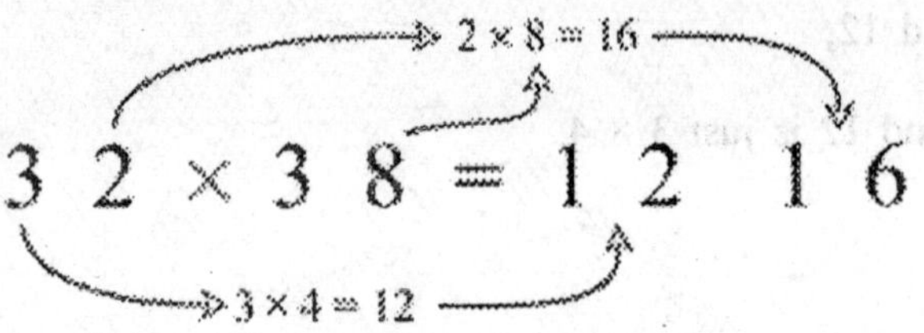

- And **81 × 89 = 7,209**

We put 09 since we need two figures as in all the other examples.

An elegant way of multiplying numbers using a simple pattern.

- **21 × 23 = 483**

This is normally called long multiplication but actually the answer can be written straight down using the VERTICALLY AND CROSSWISE formula.

We first put, or imagine, 23 below 21:

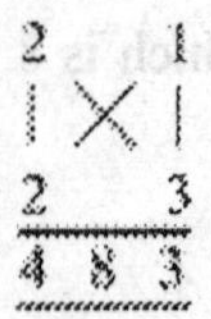

There are 3 steps:

(a) Multiply **vertically on the left:** 2 × 2 = **4.**

This gives the first figure of the answer.

(b) Multiply **crosswise and add:** 2 × 3 + 1 × 2 = **8**

This gives the middle figure.

(c) Multiply **vertically on the right:** 1 × 3 = **3**

This gives the last figure of the answer.

- Similarly **61 × 31 = 1,891**

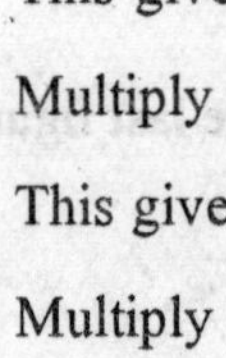

• 6 × 3 = **18**; 6 × 1 + 1 × 3 = **9**; 1 × 1 = **1**

• **33 × 44 = 1,452**

There may be more than one carry in a sum:

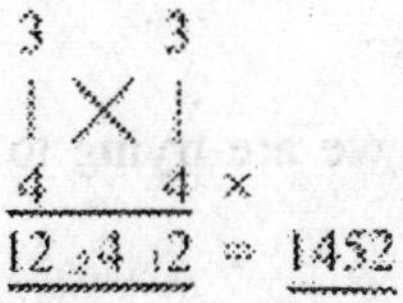

Vertically on the left we get 12. Crosswise gives us 24, so we carry 2 to the left and mentally get 144. Then vertically on the right we get 12 and the 1 here is carried over to the 144 to make 1452.

Multiplying a number by 11.

To multiply any 2-figure number by 11 we just put the total of the two figures between the 2 figures.

• **26 × 11 = 286**

Notice that the outer figures in 286 are the 26 being multiplied.

And the middle figure is just 2 and 6 added up.

• **So 72 × 11 = 792**

• **234 × 11 = 2,574**

We put the 2 and the 4 at the ends.

We add the first pair 2 + 3 = 5.

and we add the last pair: 3 + 4 = 7.

Method for diving by 9.

• **23 / 9 = 2 remainder 5**

The first figure of 23 is 2, and this is the answer.

The remainder is just 2 and 3 added up!

- **43 / 9 = 4 remainder 7**

The first figure 4 is the answer

and 4 + 3 = 7 is the remainder – could it be easier?

- **842 / 9 = 8_12 remainder 14 = 92 remainder 14**

Actually a remainder of 9 or more is not usually permitted because we are trying to find how many 9's there are in 842.

Since the remainder, 14 has one more 9 with 5 left over the final answer will be **93 remainder 5**

(1) In product of 83 & 87, digit at tenth's place is same i.e. 8 & sum of 3 & 7 is 10.

Now, follow the rules—

(a) firstly, find product of digits at unit's places i.e. here 3 * 7 = 21.

(b) secondly, multiply tenth's place digit by next consecutive number i.e. here 8 * 9 = 72.

(c) now your answer is the outcome in second step i.e. 72 followed by outcome in first step i.e.21

(d) hence, your answer is 7221.

In example 3, answer is 7 * 8 = 56 followed by 2 * 8 = 16 i.e. 5616.

You should take care that when digits at unit's places are 1 & 9, you must write their product as 09.

Considering example 4, answer is 9 * 10=90 followed by 9 * 1 = 09 i.e. 9009.

Now, you can do such specific multiplications orally within a second!

Sometime we cannot take a base 10. We will have to use another working base. For instance you wish to multiply 41*43.

We accept 100 as theoretical base and take sub multiple of 50 which is conveniently near to 41 and 43.

Note 100/2 = 50 and 50 – 9 = 41 and 50 – 7 = 43, Multiply 9 with 7 we get 63 and 43 – 9 or 41 – 7 = 34, divide 34 by 2

41 9

43 7

34/63

1,763 easy, practice more examples

Example multiple 46*46

46*46

46 4

46 4

42/16

2116

Example multiply 249*245

Our base is 1000/4 = 250

So

249 1

245 5

244/005

Divide 244 by 4 = 61

So we get 61,005

Example 77*9,988

Let us have a base of 1,000

0077 -> 9,923

9988 -> 0,012

$65/_{11}9,076$

7,69,076

7.3 RETAIL CALCULATIONS

Example 1:

You wish to find the total price of 72 items at the rate of 12

It is easy.

Cost of 72 items at the rate 10 = 720 (Just put zero after 72)

Cost of 72 items at the rate of 2 = 72 + 72 = 144

Total 720 = 144 = 864

Example 2:

You wish to calculate the value of 2,237 items at the rate of 55 paise

Value at the rate of one rupee = 2237

Value at 50 paise = 1,118.50 (Divide 2237 by 2)

Value at 5 paise = 111.85 (Divide by 10, just bring one digit to decimal side)

Add 1,118.50 + 111.85 = 1,230.35

Example 3:

You wish sell 435 items at a price of ₹ 42.39. It is very easy to calculate.

We will use three methods here.

First method

You can choose whichever you feel easy

Let us divide 435 into three parts as 400, 30 and 5. Similarly 42.39 into four or five parts as (40 + 2 + 0.30 + 0.05 + 0.04)

Items	Rate	Total	Method
400	40	16,000.00	Multiply 4 into 4 and put three zeros
	2	800.00	Multiply 2 into 4 and put two zeros
	0.3	120.00	Multiply 4 into 3 and put three zeros, put decimal after 2 digits from right to convert into rupee

0.9	36.00		
30	40	1,200.00	
2	60.00		
0.3	9.00		
0.9	2.70		
5	40	200.00	
2	10.00		
0.3	1.50		
0.9	0.45		
435	42.39	18,439.65	Total

Second Method

Add 11 paise to price to make 42.50

Cost of 400 @ 40 = 16,000

Cost of 400 @ 2.5 = 1,000

Cost of 30 items @ 40 = 1,200

Cost of 30 items @ 2.5 = 75

Cost 5 items @ 40 = 200

Cost 5 items @ 2.5 = 12.50

Total = 18,487.50

Now we added more @ 11 paise for 435 items , so at 10 paise it is 43.85 and and one paise it is 4.35. Add = 47.85

Subtract from 18,487.50 – 47.85 = 18,439.65

Third Method

Let us make simple calculations by heart

Items	Price	Total	
435	1	435	
435	10	4,350	
435	100	43,500	
435	50	21,750	Divide 43,500 by 2
435	40	17,400	21,750 – 4,350
435	20	8,700	17,400/2
435	2	870	Just remove last zero
435	0.40	174	Remove two zeros from 17,400
435	0.01	4.35	435/100
435	0.39	169.65	174 – 4.35

Now we shall total what we require

17,400 + 870 + 169.65 = 18,419

Retail management students must practice by heart. There may be many occasions when you may not get calculators.

7.4 PROBLEMS FOR PRACTICE

(Do not use calculator)

1. Find the value of 2,335 items at the rate ₹ 23.35
2. Multiply 639.39 with 479.36
3. Find the total bill amount of 3,471 items at the rate of 177.77
4. Find the salesman's commission at the rate 0.75% when he sold 245 items at the rate of ₹ 10,277.75
5. Find the total amount when 476 items were sold at ₹ 23.56, 2,100 items were sold at ₹ 127.90 and 115 items were sold at ₹ 78.80.

CHAPTER 8

Forecasting

8.1 LEARNING OBJECTIVES

After going through this chapter you will learn

(a) Introduction to regression

(b) Procedure to forecast by regression

(c) Test how far you are accurate

8.2 LINEAR REGRESSION

Regression analysis is a technique used for the modeling and analysis of numerical data consisting of values of a dependent variable (response variable) and of one or more independent variables (explanatory variables). For instance revenue has increased or decreased with advertisement. Revenue is dependent variable and advertisement exposure or expenditure is independent variable. The dependent variable in the ***regression equation*** is modeled as a function of the independent variables, corresponding parameters ("constants"), and an ***error term***. For instance Y depends upon X but it has constant and errors also. The error term is treated as a ***random variable***. It represents unexplained variation in the dependent variable. The parameters are estimated so as to give a "best fit" of the data. Most commonly the best fit is evaluated by using the least squares method, but other criteria have also been used.

When functions are established on priory assumptions which are based on theory, we may call it models. For instance Consumption is the functions of income $C = f(Y)$, we call it a model as both income (Y) and Consumption (C) are based on a theory. Data modeling can be used without there being any knowledge about the underlying processes that have generated the data; in this case the model is an empirical model. Moreover, in modeling knowledge of the probability distribution of the errors is not required. Regression analysis requires assumptions to be made regarding probability distribution of the errors. Statistical tests are made on the basis of these assumptions. In regression analysis the term "model" embraces both the function used to model the data and the assumptions concerning probability distributions.

Regression can be used for prediction (including forecasting of time series data), inference, hypothesis testing, and modeling of causal relationships. These uses of regression rely heavily on the underlying assumptions being satisfied. Regression analysis has been criticized as being misused for these purposes in many cases where the appropriate assumptions cannot be verified to hold. One factor contributing to the misuse of regression is that it can take considerably more skill to critique a model than to fit a model.

Linear regression is a form of regression analysis in which observational data are modeled by a function which is a linear combination of the model parameters and depends on one or more independent variables. In simple linear regression the model function represents a straight line. The results of data fitting are subject to statistical analysis.

The data consist of n values taken from observations (dependent or response variable), *Y*. the dependent variable is subject to error. This error is assumed to be random variable, with a mean of zero. The independent variable (explanatory variable), *X*, is assumed to be error free. If this is not so, there may be problems which needs to be rectified with various econometric techniques. The independent variables are also called regressors, exogenous variables, input variables and predictor variables. In simple linear regression the data model is written as

$$Y = \beta_0 + \beta_1 X + e$$

or

$$\hat{y} = \beta_0 + \beta_1 X$$

where e is an observational error. β_0 (intercept) and β_1 (slope) are the parameters of the model. $\hat{y}$ is the estimated Y.

Unless otherwise stated it is assumed that the observational errors are uncorrelated and belong to a normal distribution. This, or another assumption, is used when performing statistical tests on the regression results. An equivalent formulation of simple linear regression that explicitly shows the linear regression as a model of conditional expectation can be given as

$$E(y|x) = \alpha + \beta x$$

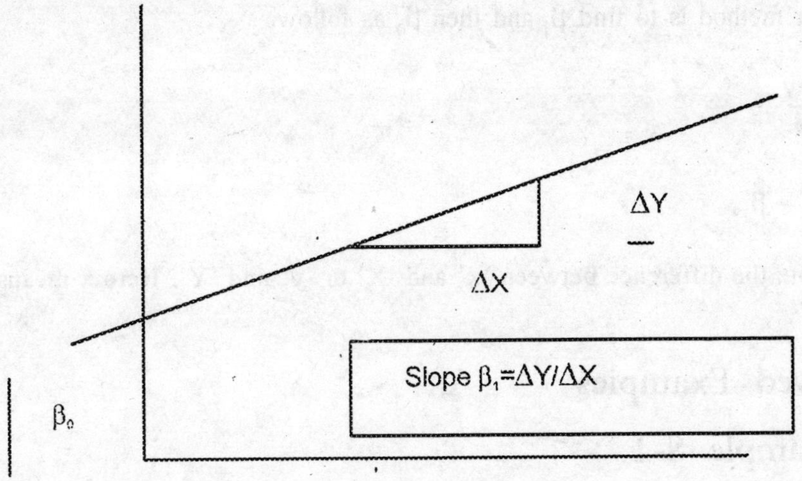

Fig. 8.1

A **trend line** represents a trend, the long-term movement in time series data after other components have been accounted for. It tells whether a particular data set (say GDP, oil prices or stock prices) have increased or decreased over the period of time. A trend line could simply be drawn by eye through a set of data points, but more properly their position and slope is calculated using statistical techniques like **linear regression**. Trend lines typically are straight lines, although some variations use higher degree polynomials depending on the degree of curvature desired in the line.

Trend lines are sometimes used in business analysis to show changes in data over time. This has the advantage of being simple. Trend lines are often used to argue that a particular action or event (such as training, or an advertising campaign) caused observed changes at a point in time. This is a simple technique, and does not require a control group, experimental design, or a sophisticated analysis technique. However, it suffers from a lack of scientific validity in cases where other potential changes can affect the data.

Staticians have suggested many methods to frame regression equation. The purpose of these formulas is to minimise the stochastic error.

β_0 is called intecept and β_1 is called slope. Slope means change in Y divided by change in X. It can also be termed as tangent of the angle opposite to perpendicular, if we show change in Y and X with a right angle triangle Fig. 8.1.

In regression, Normal Equations are written as follows

$\Sigma Y = n\,\beta_0 + \beta_1\,\Sigma X$ .... (1)

$\Sigma XY = \beta_0 \Sigma X + \beta_1\,\Sigma X^2$ ....(2)

If we calculate ΣY, ΣX, ΣXY and ΣX^2 we can find β_0, β_1

The other method is to find β_1 and then β_0 as follows

$$\beta_1 = \frac{\Sigma xy}{\Sigma x^2}$$

$$\beta_0 = \overline{Y} - \beta_{1*}$$

Please note the difference between 'x' and 'X' or 'y' and 'Y'. Here x means X– while y = Y–

8.2.1 Solved Examples

Solved example S-1

Let a company observes that when it decreases prices of its product, there is increase in sales. The observed data is as follows:

Demand	Price
28	8
33	7
38	6
47	5
52	4
56	3
61	2

Fit a regression equation and test the significance of slope and model. Also find goodness of fit.

Solution:

Let demand be Y and price be X

	Demand(Y)	Price(X)	ΣXY	ΣX^2
	28	8	224	64
	33	7	231	49
	38	6	228	36
	47	5	235	25
	52	4	208	16
	56	3	168	9

	61	2	122	4
ΣY	315			
ΣX		35		
ΣXY			1416	
ΣX^2				203

The normal equations are

$315 = 7\ \beta_0 + 35\ \beta_1$ .... (1)

$1416 = 35\beta_0 + 203\ \beta_1$ ....(2)

By solving the above equation $\beta_0 = 73.39$ and $\beta_1 = -5.6$

There regression equation is

$\hat{Y} = 73.39 - 5.678X$

or

$Y = 73.39 - 5.678X + e$

Now if the price is 8.5 we can forecast demand as

$73.39 - 5.678*8.5 = 25.127$

We shall see later how far our forecast is correct because there is error portion in model.

We can also find out β_1 by

$$\beta_1 = \frac{\Sigma xy}{\Sigma x^2}$$

Y	X	$y = Y - \bar{Y}$	$x = X - \bar{X}$	xy	χ^2	
	28	8	–17	3	–51	9
	33	7	–12	2	–24	4
	38	6	–7	1	–7	1
	47	5	2	0	0	0
	52	4	7	–1	–7	1
	56	3	11	–2	–22	4
	61	2	16	–3	–48	9
Mean Y, X	45	5	0	0	–159	28

Please note 'x' is small and is deviation of X from its mean, similarly y is small and is deviation of Y from its mean.

$$\beta_1 = \frac{\Sigma xy}{\Sigma x^2} = \frac{-159}{28} = 5.678$$

$$\beta_0 = 45 - 5.678 * 5 = 73.39$$

Hence regression equation is

$$\hat{Y} = 73.39 - 5.678X$$

or

$$Y = 73.39 - 5.678X + e$$

Now error is $Y - \hat{Y}$

Y	X	$\hat{Y}$	Error	Square of error
28	8	27.966	0.034	0.001156
33	7	33.644	–0.644	0.414736
38	6	39.322	–1.322	1.747684
47	5	45	2	4
52	4	50.678	1.322	1.747684
56	3	56.356	–0.356	0.126736
61	2	62.034	–1.034	1.069156
Sum			0	9.107152

$\Sigma e^2 = 9.1071$

(Let us understand teh concept of DF, before continueing further)

Test for regression is **goodness of fit i.e. R^2**

$$R^2 = \frac{ESS}{TSS}$$

ESS is expalained sum of square due to regression and TSS is total sum of square.

TSS = ESS + RSS

Total sum of square = Estimated Sum of Square + Residual Sum of Square

To understand, we know

$Y = \hat{Y} + e$

Substracting $\overline{Y}$ from both sides

$Y - \overline{Y} = \hat{Y} - \overline{Y} + e$

This can be written in the form of deviation as follows

$\overline{y} = \hat{y} + e$

Taking summation and square of both sides

We have

$\sum \overline{y}^2 = \sum \hat{y}^2 + \sum e^2$

TSS = ESS + RSS

Further we know

$\hat{Y} = \beta_0 + \beta_1 X$

and

$\overline{Y} = \beta_0 + \beta_{1*} \overline{X}$

therefore

$y = \beta_1 (X - \overline{X})$

$y = \beta_1 x$

Taking summation and square of both sides

$\Sigma y^2 = \beta_1{}^2 \, \Sigma x^2$

Now

TSS = ESS + RSS

$TSS = \beta_1{}^2, \Sigma x^2 + \Sigma e^2 = (5.678)^2 * 28. + 9.1071 = 911.818$

$$R^2 = \frac{ESS}{TSS} = \mathbf{(902.711)/911.818 = .99}$$

This means 99% of Y is explained by X. R^2 is considered good if it is more than .80

There are many more tests to see how far we are correct in predicting. This can also be seen with the help of charts. Draw a chart with predicted values and actual values. If actual values are near to predicted values (which is also called trend line) we can say our prediction will also be correct. See the chart below (Fig. 8.2).

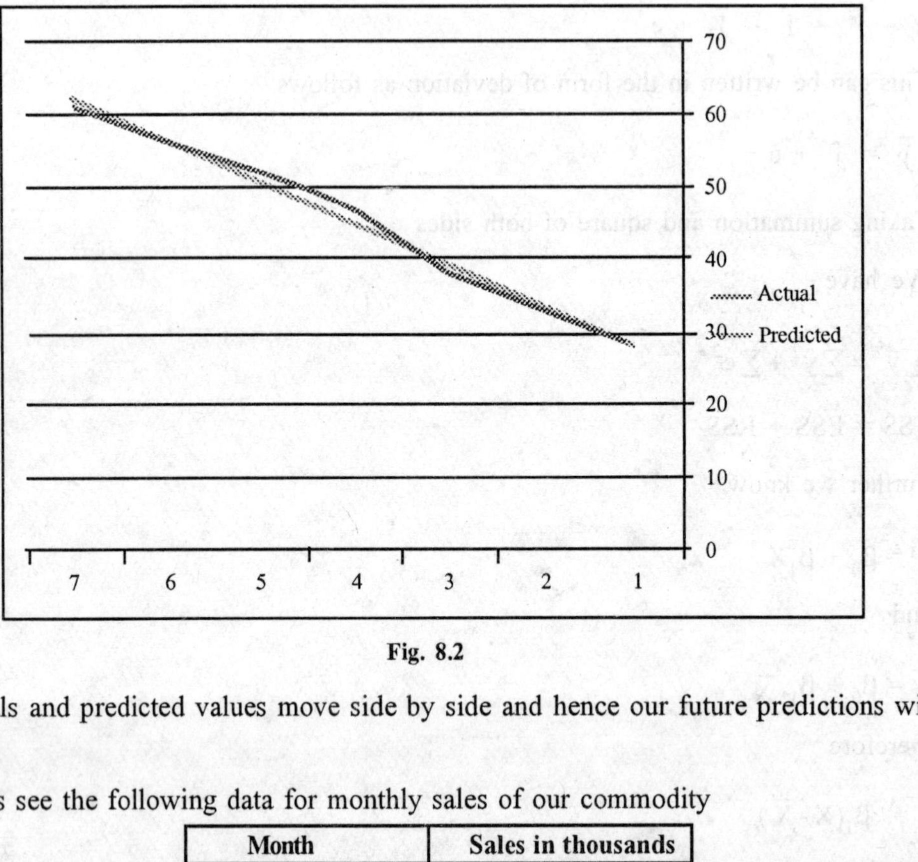

Fig. 8.2

Actuals and predicted values move side by side and hence our future predictions will not be correct.

Let us see the following data for monthly sales of our commodity

Month	Sales in thousands
1	3
2	8
3	1.5
4	9
5	3
6	15
7	1
8	12
9	13
12	2
13	20
14	12
15	8

Our regression equation will be as follows:

Sales = 4.677 + 0.280 *month

We can forecast for 20th month as 4.947 + 0.322*20 = 10.29 thousands

Now how far is this reliable?

Let us see the chart (Fig. 8.3).

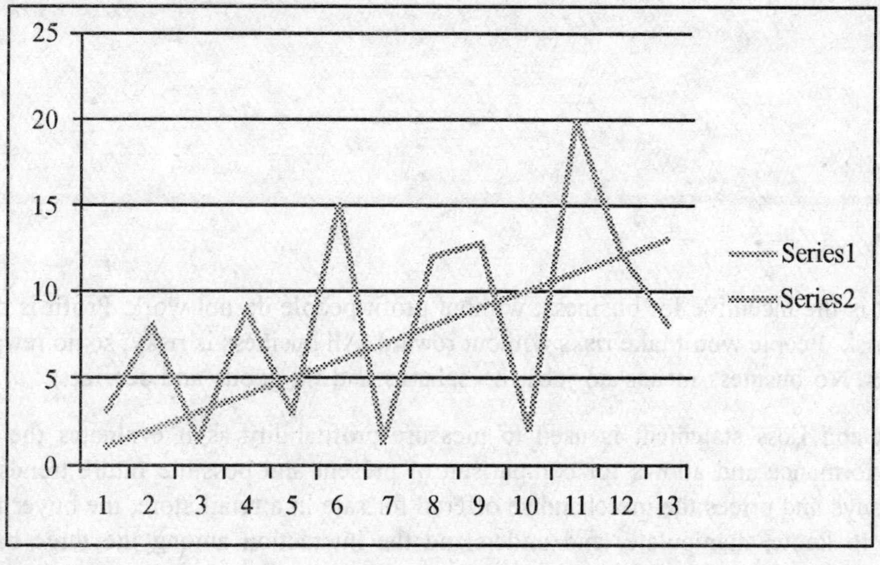

Fig. 8.3

Series 2 on shows the predicted values and series 1 shows the actual values. We can see actual values move quite away from the trend line. Therefore our forecast will not be correct. If calculate R^2, it is only 0.185 which means goodness of fit is only 18.5%, so our forecast will be correct only to the extent of 18.5%.

To read more about regression you should read a good book on econometrics or Business Research Methodology by J.K. SACHDEVA, published by Himalaya Publishing House, Mumbai.

ଔଔଔ

CHAPTER 9

Summary

Profit is the incentive for business; without profit people do not work. Profit is the reward for taking risk. People won't take risks without reward. All business is risky, so no reward means no business. No business means no jobs, no salaries and no goods and services.

Profit and Loss statement is used to measure profitability as it evaluates the results of current performance and allows for comparison of present and possible future trends. Because the buyer buys and prices the merchandise offered for sale in a retail store, the buyer must have the ability to know, manipulate, and understand the interaction among the three basic profit factors, which are:

1. the operating income, also known as sales or sales volume, which indicates in rupees how much merchandise has been sold;
2. the cost of goods sold, which shows the amount paid for the goods sold;
3. and the operating expenses, which refers to those expenses, other than the cost of the goods, incurred in the buying/selling process.

Breakeven analysis is a technique widely used by production management and management accountants. However, it is widely used by retailers also. It is based on categorising procurement costs between those which are "variable" (costs that change when the quantity of sales changes) and those that are "fixed" (costs not directly related to the volume of sale).

From the breakeven analysis, we can say that there are only three ways to increase profit:

- Increase your sales volumes.
- Increase your sales prices.
- Reduce your costs.

Price in business is the result of an exchange and from that trade we assign a numerical monetary value to a good, service or asset. Price is only part of the information we get from observing an exchange. The other part is the volume of the goods traded per unit time, called the rate of purchase or sale. From this additional information we understand the extent of the market and the elasticity of the demand and supply.

A buyer creates a stock assortment by considering what price lines to carry and the depth of assortment offered at the various price points. The number of price lines, and those particular price lines in the assortments, can help reflect the desired character that management wishes to project. The emphasis of a stock by price lines depends on the composition of the consumer segment that management wishes to attract. Usually, there is a price structure around which buying for a specific retail establishment is concentrated.

Markup is the amount that is added to the cost price of merchandise to arrive at a retail price. This amount must be large enough to cover the cost of the merchandise, the expenses incurred to sell it and the desired profit. The dynamic nature of merchandising makes the repricing of goods in retailing universal. Price adjustments are made to either increase or decrease the original retail price placed on merchandise.

The most common and important type of price adjustment is technically called markdown (MD). It is the lowering or reducing of the original or previous retail price on one item or a group of items. Markdowns are "a cure, not a curse." This merchandising tool can be used to good advantage if the retailer realizes the objectives of markdowns.

Employee Discounts is common practice for a retail store to give its employees a reduction off a retail price. This reduction is generally stated as a percentage off the retail price. It must be recorded by the statistical department of the accounting division for accuracy of the book inventory figure under the retail method of inventory. The cumulative amount of employees' discounts is usually shown on the profit and loss statement under the general heading of "retail reductions."

Price adjustments in retailing is impossible, stores must classify each type of adjustment separately so that they can be analyzed, planned, and controlled. Markdowns, the major type of price changes, reduce the retail price, causing a decrease in gross margin that is further reflected in a decrease and/or elimination of profit. With certain merchandise or classifications, the markdown risk is frequently anticipated. It is offset by planning a higher initial (original) markup.

Unfortunately, profit cannot always be preplanned because there are business forces that do not permit easy solutions to problems (e.g., non acceptance of a newly introduced fashion or style, change in competition, etc.).

Initial markup is the difference between the billed cost of merchandise and the original or first retail price placed on a given item or group of items. When freight charges are known, they are added to the billed cost when calculating initial markup.

Cumulative markup is the markup percentage achieved on all goods available for sale from the beginning of a given period. It is an average markup because it is the markup percentage obtained on the accumulated inventory at the beginning of the given period, plus the markup of all the new purchases received season to date. The cumulative markup in rupees equals the difference between the invoiced cost of the merchandise (including transportation) before cash discounts have been adjusted and the cumulative original retail prices of all merchandise handled (opening inventory + net purchases) during a given period of time. Markdowns do not enter into the calculation of the cumulative markup percentage.

Averaging markups means adjusting the proportions of goods purchased at different markups, to achieve the desired aggregate markup, either for an individual purchase or for a certain period. In merchandising the purchases, the buyer builds a "cushion" or lowers the markup depending on the situation. This practice is prevalent in the fashion and fashion related industries.

Inventory levels constantly change. As goods are purchased or produced, inventories increase. As goods are sold, inventories are reduced. To determine the inventory at the end of any period, you begin with the inventory on hand at the beginning of the period. Inventory calculations, based upon units, are useful when determining the inventory of a particular item. More often, however, you will want to know the rupee value of inventory, particularly your total inventory. Total inventory can be evaluated in total rupee s only since it usually includes a mix of various items such as apples and oranges, which cannot be added together.

The retail system of merchandise accounting permits the retailer to determine the value (at retail) of the stock on hand at frequent and periodic intervals with out taking constant physical counts. However, it must be noted that periodic— generally semi annual—physical counts (i.e., inventories) are taken at the current retail prices of the merchandise on hand.

To control stocks and determine the profitability of individual departments, the retail method of accounting is applied separately for each department. Physical inventories at current retail prices are taken at the end of the accounting period. At this same time, the "book stock" at retail is adjusted to agree with the value of the physical count. Any discrepancy between the amount of the "book stock" and the value of stock determined by the physical count of merchandise on hand is classified as a shortage (or shrinkage) or an overage.

Merchandise control results from effective use of data that is available through the rupee planning procedure. In purchasing merchandise, a buyer is guided by the timing and quantity goals established in the six month seasonal rupee plan. To provide an even tighter control on the amount of merchandise received in a specific period and to achieve as precisely as possible the sales and stock plans, the buyer refers to a merchandising figure called OPEN-TO-BUY.

A product is first sold by a manufacturer to one or more distributors. The agreement between a manufacturer and a distributor usually gives the distributor the exclusive right to distribute the product in a fairly large geographic region. The manufacturer sometimes prohibits the distributor from handling competing products. Typically, a distributor also has marketing responsibilities in the region. The distributor then resells the goods to a number of wholesalers.